Fruit!

Fruit!

Fresh and delicious recipes for sweet and main dishes

Kathryn Hawkins

Good Books

Intercourse, PA 17534
800/762-7171
www.GoodBooks.com

Dedication
In memory of my father, Terry.

This edition copyright © 2008 by Good Books, Intercourse,
PA 17534

International Standard Book Number: 978-1-56148-593-2
(paperback edition)
International Standard Book Number: 978-1-56148-594-9
(comb-bound edition)
Library of Congress Catalog Card Number: 2007004328

Text and recipe copyright © 2007 Kathryn Hawkins
Photographs copyright © 2007 New Holland Publishers (UK) Ltd
Copyright © 2007 New Holland Publishers (UK) Ltd

Library of Congress Cataloging-in-Publication Data

Hawkins, Kathryn
     Fruit! : fresh and delicious recipes for sweet and main
dishes / Kathryn Hawkins
         p. cm.
     Includes index.
     ISBN-13: 978-1-56148-593-2 (pbk. : alk. paper)
     ISBN-13: 978-1-56148-594-9 (comb-bound : alk.paper)
     1. Cookery (Fruit)   2. Fruit.   I. Title
     TX811.H39 2007
     641.6'4--dc22
                              2007004328

Editor: Ruth Hamilton
Copy Editor: Anna Bennett
Design: Paul Wright
Photography: Stuart West
Food Styling: Stella Murphy
Production: Hazel Kirkman
Editorial Direction: Rosemary Wilkinson

Reproduction by Pica Digital PTD Ltd, Singapore
Printed and bound by C&C Offset Printing, China

Acknowledgments
Special thanks go to my mother Margaret for her continued
support and her help with recipe testing in such difficult
circumstances; to Craig and Liz Copland, Malcolm and Ross,
and everyone at the Handy Shop in Crieff, for their help in
finding the produce for my recipe testing; to my partner Stuart,
and other friends and family who offered encouragement and
ideas, and helped out with the tasting. Thanks also go to Clare
Hubbard for her support throughout the project, and to Stella
Murphy and Stuart West for bringing the recipes to life.

The publisher would like to thank Denby for supplying the props
used throughout the book.

Contents

Introduction

For centuries, fruit has inspired
artists to put brush to canvas,
and moved poets, literary writers
and, of course, food writers to put
pen to paper and wax lyrical on a
food category that appeals to the
senses like no other. I first started
work on this book during the
depths of a very cold and dreary
Scottish winter, and it was
wonderful to be thinking about
the spectrum of colors, the
different shapes, sizes, textures,
aromas and flavors of the
hundreds of fruits available today.
It made me think that fruits are
the most beautiful of all foods and
that a life devoid of them would
be very dull and lackluster.

The Chambers dictionary defines
"fruit" as: "an edible part of a
plant, generally sweet, acid,
and juicy, esp. a part that
contains the seed." Botanically
speaking, the word "fruit" also
covers non-sweet foods such
as tomato, avocado and
peppers but, in culinary terms,
these foods are used primarily as
vegetables. Nuts and some
spices such as peppercorns are

also, technically, "fruits," but with so much to cover, this book would have ended up as an unwieldy tome rather than a handy cookbook! For the purposes of this book, therefore, I have looked at a wide variety of fruits and put together a collection of recipes alongside a useful reference section on those that are most readily available. You'll find plenty of ideas and information on how to prepare different fruits; tips on choosing the perfect fruit and how best to store it; how to preserve the flavors for year-round enjoyment, and, of course, lots of recipes to tempt you to cook fruit in different ways. Being a very versatile food, fruit can be used in both savory and sweet dishes and you'll find recipes showing you how to use different fruits to their best advantage, and which flavors are most complementary. You'll find classic recipes for pies, cakes and jams alongside more contemporary recipes: a mixture of old favorites and lighter modern-day counterparts to suit current trends in healthy eating.

Nutritionally speaking, fruit is a wonder food. Not only does it taste great and make you feel wonderful, but it's also packed full of antioxidants, vitamins and minerals to enrich your diet. Vitamin C is present in all fruit in varying degrees; orange, yellow and red-fleshed fruits have higher vitamin A (carotene) contents than most other fruits, and with fruits where the skins and seeds are eaten, you'll be ingesting more dietary fiber than in peeled and seedless fruit. There's little or no fat in fruit so you don't have to worry about cholesterol or saturates, making it a dieter's staple. The natural sweetness comes from fructose, one of the most digestible and satisfying of all sugars. It gently enters the blood-stream and is easily absorbed without giving the unsatisfactory sugar-fueled charge produced by pure sucrose.

Today we are faced with an enormous variety of different fruits on the shelf. Once people began to travel the world and settle in foreign locations, they started to

import produce from their country of origin and soon the local diet began to incorporate more exotic fruit. With the boom in import and export, the world has become a much smaller place, and exotic produce is flown from one side of the world to another in order to satisfy consumer demand. New varieties are being developed all the time to keep up with the ever-changing tastes of the 21st-century consumer. Seedless and easy-peel fruits have been developed for our convenience; growers have been encouraged to develop fruits that can be grown for longer seasons so that we can have fruits like strawberries on our table year-round. Varieties have been developed to suit different climates and to resist disease, and, for mass production, fruit is grown in uniform shapes and sizes for easier packing and to meet regulations. But what does this really mean for the consumer? The truth is that fruit grown out of season, force-grown out of its natural climate, doesn't really have the best flavor, and, with current worries over climate control and air/food miles, perhaps it would be better if we started enjoying fruit in its natural season, and more locally grown. With this in mind, it is exciting to hear about the resurgence in interest in ancient fruit species from our culinary heritage, which are being rediscovered and are increasingly available for us to grow. If you've got the time to garden then you'll be lucky enough to taste and see the difference in flavor and shape. For those of us who are time-challenged, it's worth checking out your local greengrocer. Another suggestion is to make the most of local farm shops and pick-your-own places if available; these outlets are likely to grow different, sometimes local varieties, and the produce will be fresher and not far traveled.

I've very much enjoyed putting this book together. It's given me the opportunity to work with some of my favorite ingredients and to experiment with ones that were less familiar to me. I hope you like reading the book and become inspired to cook some of your favorite fruits in different ways and perhaps try some new ones as well.

Choosing, preparing and storing fruit

CHOOSING PERFECTLY RIPE FRUIT

If you actually stop and think about why fruit is so attractive, you realize that Mother Nature is very clever indeed. Fruit is the part of the plant that is specifically designed to attract animals to eat it and then disperse the seeds, and thus multiply. For this reason, fruit has to be attention-grabbing, so visually attractive that once noticed, it will be tempting enough to be eaten. You only have to think of Adam and Eve and *that* apple to see what I'm getting at!

Once you've gotten past the basics, the science behind the general appeal is very interesting. When a fruit begins to develop, it is nothing more than a vegetable – it is more than likely to be green and not sweet at all. It must be ripe in order to meet our conditioned expectations. The ripening begins during the final stages of fruit development when an enzyme called *ethylene*, triggered by a hormone, encourages the fruit to start storing sugar in its cells; defensive compounds which protect the developing fruit against infection – and, by their astringent nature, deter predators – begin to decrease in numbers. As the sugar content increases and the compound levels decline, the texture of the fruit softens, the color changes to an attractive shade – yellow, orange, red or purple – and the aroma develops. Now the fruit is acceptable and attractive enough to be eaten.

Different fruit ripens at different rates. When the ripening reaction takes place rapidly, the fruit carries on ripening at such a rate that, if not picked in time, will soon go past its best and begin to rot. Fruits where this process occurs are categorized as *climacteric* and include bananas, pears and kiwi fruit. Fortunately for us, these fruits can be harvested before they have finished ripening. They will either continue to ripen on their own or can be helped along the way by artificially gassing them with a dose of ethylene. Early harvested fruit will of course be firmer and therefore easier to pack and transport. This means that the fruit arrives on our shelves in perfect condition and can be enjoyed when perfectly ripe. You can ripen fruit yourself using the ethylene produced from a piece of fruit that is already ripe. Place the ripe and unripe fruits together in a paper bag (not a plastic one, which will only make the fruit "sweat"). The ripe fruit will then stimulate the unripe fruit to ripen. However, take care when you store *ripe* fruits with ethylene-producing fruit, as fruit will quickly decay and shrivel – make sure you don't store sensitive produce next to ethylene-sensitive fruits (or vegetables) for long periods of time. The following lists will help you with any storage dilemmas:

Ethylene producers:
apple, apricot, ripe banana, fig, guava, ripe kiwi fruit, mango, melon (but not watermelon), nectarine, papaya, passion fruit, peach, pear, quince, persimmon.

Ethylene sensitive:
unripe banana, unripe kiwi fruit, watermelon; also green vegetables, carrots, cauliflower, peppers (capsicums), salad leaves, squash and sweet potatoes.

Fruits that are slower to ripen are called *non-climacteric* and include melons, pineapples, citrus fruit and most berries. They are unable to store the sugar and need continuous "feeding" from the plant in order to ripen completely. Such fruits need to be carefully judged when they are perfectly ripe and then expertly picked and packed. At the point of sale, use your senses to tell whether the fruit looks good enough to eat. The color will attract your attention if it pleases your eye; if you handle the fruit before purchase, it should yield slightly to light pressure – this shows you that is soft and juicy enough to eat. And, finally, perfectly ripe fruit should have its own unique aroma which tempts you to eat it. The aroma comes from chemicals called *esters*. These are made up of acids and alcohols that are bound together by plant enzymes, which give each fruit its own particular flavor/smell. So next time you go to buy fruit, remember that your senses are part of a very clever and well-devised scientific plan.

STEP-BY-STEP FRUIT PREPARATION

At first glance, you might think this section is surplus to your requirements. But during my research I thought it would be a good idea to put together a set of instructions for preparing certain fruits to ensure you get the best from them with minimum fuss and waste.

Citrus

This method can be used if you want to segment the fruit or serve it in slices without the skin. Using a sharp knife, slice the top and bottom off the fruit. Slice off the peel, taking away as much of the white pith as possible. You can now slice the fruit into thin round slices or keep it whole. For segments, hold the peeled fruit over a bowl to catch the juices and slice in between each segment to remove the flesh, allowing the segments to fall into the bowl.

Dates

Using a small, sharp knife, cut through the date lengthways, working around the stone until you have two neat halves. Prize the stone out of the fruit with the tip of the knife.

Kiwi

I have always found it difficult to peel a ripe kiwi fruit using a vegetable peeler. Instead, I cut a small slice from the top and bottom of the fruit; I then use a curved-blade paring knife to cut off the brown hairy skin very thinly in downward slices. Cut in half, quarters or slices.

Mango

The smooth, flat stone of the mango lies lengthways through the center of the fruit. Slice down either side of the stone, running the knife as close to it as possible. Cut each slice in half and run the knife between the skin and the flesh to remove as much flesh as possible. Cut away any remaining flesh from the stone and peel away the skin. Slice, cube or cut into wedges as desired.

Papaya

I prefer to cut papayas in half before peeling them. Using a teaspoon, scoop out the black round seeds. Carefully peel off the skin using a vegetable peeler or small sharp knife. Slice, cube or cut into wedges as desired.

Passion fruit

I find it easier to pierce the thick skin of passion fruit with the tip of a sharp knife before attempting to slice in half. Scoop the pulp out from the skin using a teaspoon.

Pineapple

Slice the top and bottom off the pineapple. Stand it upright on a cutting board and, using a sharp knife, cut the skin off in downward slices, working your way around the fruit. For slices, cut into thin round slices and remove the central core by pressing out using a small round cookie cutter or apple corer. For wedges, cut the pineapple lengthways into quarters, and slice off the core from each piece.

Pomegranate

To obtain as much juice as possible from a pomegranate, allow it to stand at room temperature for a while rather than using it straight from the fridge. Roll the fruit gently backwards and forwards across the work surface a few times to loosen the juice in the segments (this method also works well with citrus fruit). Cut the fruit in half widthways. For juicing, press the fruit onto a citrus reamer rather than twisting it to release the juice. Remember that pomegranate juice stains, so take care with splashing juice. Pass through a fine mesh sieve to remove any bits of seed or membrane. To use the seeds, simply prize out into a bowl using a teaspoon.

Stoned fruit (apricots, peaches, plums and nectarines)

Using a small sharp knife, cut around the fruit deep enough to just touch the stone with the knife. Gently twist the halves in opposite directions to release them from the stone. Carefully prize out the stone with the tip of the knife or your fingers.

FRUIT STORAGE AND PRESERVATION

As we all know, fruit does not keep very well and soon passes its best. Whole, uncut fruit should be stored at room temperature, in a cool space, well ventilated (in a rack or shallow fruit bowl), out of direct sunlight. If the fruit is becoming over-ripe, it can be refrigerated to delay the action, but should be used as soon as possible. If bananas are refrigerated the skin will blacken – the flesh will be fine, though. Cut fruit should be wrapped in plastic wrap to prevent drying, and then stored in the fridge – once again, use as quickly as possible.

If you buy pre-packed berries, remove them from the containers and remove any damaged fruit.

If not using immediately, leave them unwashed and place in a single layer on a plate or shallow bowl, cover with plastic wrap and refrigerate. Use as soon as possible, washing before use. Grapes and cherries should be kept in the fridge until needed.

In times gone by, before modern preservation techniques such as refrigeration, freezing and canning, cooks would capture the flavors of each different season by making various jams, jellies, pickles, vinegars and chutneys, and therefore enjoy a collection of fruits all year round. In the final chapter of this book, I have collected several classic recipes to show you different ways in which fruit can be preserved. Here are a few basic techniques that will ensure you have successful results.

Choosing fruit

It is essential that you start with the best-quality produce in order to prevent further deterioration during storage. Fruit should be perfectly ripe (unless the recipe states otherwise), blemish-free, free from mold and mildew, and correctly prepared prior to being used in a recipe.

Cooking

Fruit is often simmered, either on its own or with liquid, before sugar is added. Cook the fruit slowly, keeping the pan uncovered (unless otherwise stated) and stirring occasionally until just softened. This will allow you to obtain the maximum amount of juice from the fruit. If the juice yielded is scant, add a bit more water – this can occur if the fruit is firmer than usual. Take care not to overcook the fruit at this stage, otherwise flavor and color will be impaired.

Testing for the setting point

There are two main ways that I use to find out if a preserve has reached the setting point:

1) Using a sugar thermometer – for jam, marmalade, conserves and fruit butter, an acceptable reading range should be from 219–222°F (104–105.5°C). The lower temperature will give a softer set than the higher one – used for conserves. Use the higher temperature for fruit butters. For jellies, use 219–221°F (104–105°C).

2) The wrinkle test – take the saucepan of boiling preserve off

the heat and quickly spoon a little preserve onto a cold flat plate; allow to cool. If the preserve is ready, a slight skin will form on the surface and it will wrinkle when pushed with your finger. Return the saucepan to a boil if the preserve isn't ready and test again in the same way in about 2 minutes.

Preparing storage jars and bottles

Use glass containers that are free from cracks or chips. Wash thoroughly in very hot water with mild detergent and rinse well. Dry with a clean cloth. Place on a baking tray lined with a few layers of paper towel and keep warm in the oven on the lowest setting.

Filling the jars

A clean ladle or small heatproof measuring cup will be useful to help you transfer the preserve to the prepared jar or bottle. If the preserve is very fruity, or contains rind and small pieces, stir it well before putting in the jars. Fill to within ¼in (6mm) of the top of the jar. Half-filled jars of preserve should be cooled, sealed and kept in the fridge and eaten as soon as possible.

Sealing

To prevent spoiling during storage it is essential to have an airtight seal on your preserves. Pour into sterile canning jars and seal, following the lid manufacturer's instructions.

Storage

Don't forget to label your preserve jars with their contents and date when they were made. Keep in a cool, dry, dark place in order to preserve their color and quality. If perfectly prepared and stored, most jams, jellies and marmalades will keep for up to 12 months; chutneys, pickles and vinegars for around 6-8 months; and fruit butters for up to 6 months. See specific recipes for other storage instructions.

FREEZING

Without a doubt, freezing is the most effective way to preserve fruit. Most fruits will keep for up to 12 months in the freezer giving you year-round enjoyment – particularly good if you have a glut of garden produce. Choose only top-quality, ripe, fresh fruit for freezing – slightly over-ripe fruit can be frozen in purée form. Specific instructions for individual fruits are given in the glossary section of this book (see pages 158–170), but here are some general instructions.

Preparation

Wash unpeeled fruit well and remove leaves and stalks. Pat dry thoroughly, using paper towel, in order to prevent too much ice forming during freezing and individual fruits sticking together in a solid lump.

Open-freezing

This is a particularly suitable method for freezing berries or pieces of fruit. Lay on trays lined with baking parchment and place in the freezer until solid. Either seal in freezer bags, trying to expel as much air out of the bag as possible, or pack in rigid containers with fitted lids. Label and store until required. Freezing fruit in this way will enable you to take out small quantities from the bag at a time because the fruit shouldn't stick together once frozen and packed.

Purée and pulp

Raw, ripe fruit such as berries, mangoes and bananas can be puréed and packed into small rigid containers to freeze. If smaller quantities are required, freeze in ice cube trays and then transfer to freezer bags – you can then defrost small amounts as necessary. Fruit purée that discolors, such as banana, should be mixed with a little lemon juice or sugar to prevent browning. Purée is excellent for making sauces for ice cream and fruit coulis. Cooked fruit can also be puréed down and frozen in the same way – stewed apples, plums and apricots freeze well in a purée. Fruit with pulp such as passion fruit or pomegranate can be scooped into ice cube trays to freeze and placed in freezer bags once frozen.

Freezing in sugar

Use approximately 3–4oz (90–125g) extra-fine sugar per 1lb (500g) fruit, depending on how sweet the fruit is. As you layer the prepared fruit in its container, sprinkle lightly with sugar. On defrosting, the sugar will make its own juice. This is a good way to preserve a mixture of berries, because once they defrost, you have a ready-made compôte or topping for a cheesecake.

Freezing in syrup

Some fruits, such as peaches and apricots, discolor easily and so a light sugar syrup is useful in order to prevent this. You can make up the sugar syrup as described on page 144, allow to cool completely and stir in 2 Tbsp lemon juice. Pack the prepared fruit into rigid freezer containers and pour over the syrup. Place a piece of baking parchment directly on top of the fruit in order to keep the fruit pieces submerged before you put the lid on. Label and store until required.

Apples and pears

Some of our favorite and best-known recipes center around apples and pears – top of the list being apple pie. Along with quinces, these fruits are among the most recognized throughout history, and feature in recipes dating back hundreds of years.

In this chapter I've included a few classics such as Deep-dish apple pie (see page 21), together with some more contemporary ways to use apples in order to suit modern tastes and the trend towards healthier eating, as in Fragrant poached apples (see page 22).

I love baking, so the Apple and cheese scones (see page 24) and Chocolate pear cake (see page 29) are personal favorites in this chapter. Quince is a fruit that I have rediscovered in recent years and now use as much as apples when they are in season in the autumn. I like the firmer texture and distinct, more aromatic flavor. Quince retains its texture well during cooking, so it is perfect in dishes such as Spiced red cabbage with quince (see page 33) or when mixed with sliced apples in a classic Apple and quince Brown Betty (see page 23).

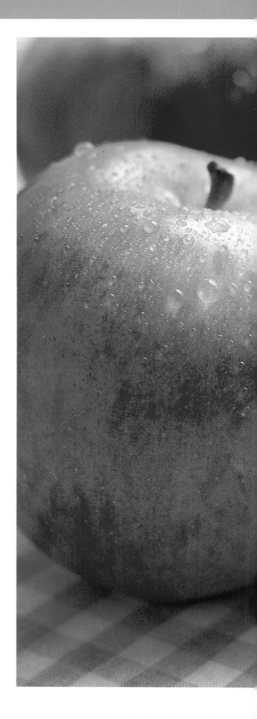

Deep-dish apple pie

Deep-dish apple pie

Sunday lunch

Everyone loves a slice of apple pie, and it always goes down well no matter what the occasion. This is my favorite recipe because there's lots of apple in the filling, delicately flavored with spices and lemon.

Serves 6 to 8

2 quantities **pastry (see Fresh lime tart recipe, page 94) or 1½lb (750g) ready-made pie pastry**
2lb (1kg) **cooking apples**
Finely grated rind and juice of 1 **large lemon**
¾ cup (125g) light brown sugar
2 Tbsp **cornstarch**
1½ tsp **ground pumpkin pie spice**
½ cup (60g) **golden raisins**
¼ stick (30g) **unsalted butter**
1 **egg white,** beaten
1 Tbsp **extra-fine sugar**

To serve:
Custard sauce (see page 145), ice cream or light cream

Preheat the oven to 375°F/190°C. Prepare the pastry as directed on page 94. Roll out two-thirds of the pastry on a lightly floured surface and use to line a 9-in (23-cm) round springform cake pan. Chill for 30 minutes.

Meanwhile, peel, core and thinly slice the apples. Place in a bowl and toss in the lemon rind and juice. In another bowl, mix the brown sugar, cornstarch and pumpkin pie spice together.

Sprinkle a little of the sugar mixture over the base of the pie crust, and mix the remainder into the apples together with the raisins. Pack down into the pie crust and dot the top with the butter.

Roll out the remaining pastry to fit the top of the pie. Brush the pie edge with a little egg white and press the pie lid on top. Trim and seal the edges. Using a sharp knife, make a small hole in the center of the pie lid so that the steam can escape. Place a baking sheet in the oven for 5 minutes.

Brush the top of the pie with egg white and sprinkle with extra-fine sugar. Set the springform pan on the hot baking sheet and bake for 45–50 minutes until the apples are tender – push a skewer into the center to see if they are cooked – and the top is golden. Stand for 10 minutes before unclipping the pan. Serve the pie hot or cold, with Custard sauce (see page 145), ice cream or light cream.

Fragrant poached apples

Perfumed

Pears in red wine is a classic dessert, and here I have applied the same cooking method to apples. It works very well and gives the apples a light pinkish blush.

Serves 4

¾ cup (150ml) **water**
4 Tbsp **extra-fine sugar**
4 **eating apples**
1 Tbsp **lemon juice**
⅔ cup (150ml) **sweet rosé wine**
1 **vanilla pod**
1 tsp **rosewater**

To serve:
Whipped cream or plain yogurt

Pour the water into a saucepan and add the sugar. Heat gently, stirring until dissolved. Bring to a boil and simmer for 5 minutes.

Meanwhile, peel the apples, leaving them whole, with stalks intact. Brush all over with lemon juice to prevent browning. Place in a medium saucepan, arranging the apples so they sit snugly side by side, and pour over the wine and the hot syrup. Bring to a boil, then cover and simmer gently for 15 minutes. Turn the apples over and cook for a further 10 minutes until just tender.

Remove from the heat, add the vanilla pod and set aside to cool. Discard the pod and stir in the rosewater. Transfer to a serving bowl, cover and chill for 2 hours. Serve with whipped cream or plain yogurt.

Apple and quince Brown Betty

Traditional

Here's my version of a classic family pudding. You can use only apples if you prefer. Delicious with my Custard sauce (see page 145).

Serves 4 to 6

3⅓ cups (200g) **fresh whole-wheat breadcrumbs**
1 stick (100g) **butter**
¾ cup (125g) **light brown sugar**
14oz (400g) **cooking apples**
10oz (300g) **quince**
Finely grated rind and juice
1 **large lemon**
½ tsp **ground cinnamon**
¼ tsp **ground nutmeg**
4 Tbsp **unsweetened apple juice**

Preheat the oven to 350°F/180°C. Place the breadcrumbs in a heatproof bowl. Melt the butter and stir into the crumbs together with half the sugar. Spoon half the mixture into the bottom of a 6¼-cup (1.5-L) ovenproof dish. Set aside.

Peel and core the apples and quince. Slice thinly and place in a bowl. Toss in the lemon rind and juice, spices and remaining sugar. Mix well and pile into the dish. Spoon over the apple juice. Top with the remaining breadcrumbs and stand on a baking dish. Bake for about 50 minutes until tender – test the center with a skewer to check if it is cooked. Serve hot with Custard sauce (see page 145).

Apple and cheese scones

Home baking

These smell wonderful when they're baking. For best results, use a strongly flavored or sharp cheese – blue cheese is good too. Serve warm, with lots of butter.

Makes 6

2 cups (250g) **self-rising flour**
1 **pinch salt**
2 tsp **baking powder**
¼ stick (30g) **unsalted butter**
4oz (125g) **mature Cheddar cheese,** grated
2 **eating apples**
1 Tbsp **wholegrain mustard**
1 **egg,** beaten
Approx. 2–3 Tbsp **unsweetened apple juice**

Preheat the oven to 400°F/200°C. Sift the flour, salt and baking powder into a bowl and rub in the butter. Stir in the cheese.

Peel and core the apples, and grate coarsely. Stir into the mixture along with the mustard, half the beaten egg and enough apple juice to bind the mixture together into a soft dough.

On a lightly floured surface, gently roll out or press the dough into a round about ¾in (2cm) thick. Using a 3½-in (8-cm) plain round cutter, stamp out six rounds, re-rolling the trimmings as necessary.

Transfer to a baking sheet, brush the tops with the remaining beaten egg and bake for 15–18 minutes until risen and golden. Place on a wire rack to cool. Best served warm, split in half and buttered.

Apple and cheese scones

Pear and ginger cheesecake

Pear and ginger cheesecake

Creamy

This is adapted from a recipe my sister-in-law Sarah makes with apples and hazelnuts. Simply replace the pears with apples, and use plain cookies in the base, replacing 2oz (60g) of the cookies with ground, toasted hazelnuts.

Serves 8

½ stick (60g) **unsalted butter**
6oz (180g) **ginger cookies,** crushed
1 cup (250g) **full-fat cream cheese**
1 cup (250g) **mascarpone**
Finely grated rind of 1 **lemon**
1 Tbsp **lemon juice**
2 **eggs,** beaten
½ cup (125g) **extra-fine sugar**
12oz (350g) **ripe pears,** peeled, cored and thinly sliced

To serve:
Light cream
Fruit coulis (see page 155)

Preheat the oven to 300°F/150°C. Grease and line an 8-in (20-cm) springform cake pan. Melt the butter in a saucepan. Remove from the heat and stir in the crushed cookies. Press the mixture into the base of the pan using the back of a spoon. Chill until required.

In a mixing bowl, beat the cream cheese and mascarpone together until soft. Stir in the lemon rind and juice, and whisk in the eggs and sugar. Gently stir in the pears until well mixed.

Transfer to the pan and set on a baking sheet. Bake for about 1½ hours, covering the top lightly with foil if it begins to brown too quickly, until firm and set. Turn off the heat, leave the oven door ajar, and allow the cheesecake to cool in the oven.

Carefully remove from the pan, transfer to a serving plate and chill for 2 hours before serving. Serve with light cream and Fruit coulis (see page 155).

Roast pear tart with coffee sauce

Contemporary

Coffee-flavored desserts are not often found on most menus, and I'm always looking for new ideas. This creamy coffee sauce is the perfect partner for ripe pears and crisp pastry.

Serves 6

8 small ripe pears
Juice of 1 lemon
4 Tbsp honey
¾ stick (90g) unsalted butter
14oz (400g) ready-made puff pastry

For the sauce:
½ stick (60g) unsalted butter
½ cup (125g) extra-fine sugar
½ cup (125g) corn syrup
4 tsp coffee extract
⅔ cup (150ml) heavy cream

Preheat the oven to 400°F/200°C. Peel and halve the pears. Place in a shallow roasting pan and toss in the lemon juice. Drizzle over the honey and dot with butter. Bake for about 30 minutes until tender, basting occasionally. Allow to cool.

Increase the oven temperature to 425°F/220°C. Roll out the pastry on a lightly floured surface to a rectangle 9 x 14in (24 x 36cm). Transfer to a large baking sheet, lined with baking parchment. Prick the base thoroughly all over with a fork and bake for about 10 minutes until lightly golden.

Drain the pears, reserving the juices, and arrange in two neat rows over the pastry base. Drizzle with the reserved juices and bake for a further 10 minutes until hot.

For the sauce, place the butter, sugar and syrup in a saucepan and heat gently, stirring, until melted and the sugar has dissolved. Stir in the coffee extract and cream and reheat until hot – do not boil.

When you are ready to serve, gently reheat the sauce if necessary, slice the tart and serve warm with the coffee sauce.

Chocolate pear cake

Indulgent

Pears marry with chocolate in the same way strawberries and cream do –
it's a winning combination. This dense, rich cake is best eaten the day after
it is baked so that the flavors and texture have had time to develop fully.

Serves 8–10

1 stick (125g) **unsalted butter,**
  softened
¾ cup (125g) **dark brown sugar**
2 **large eggs,** beaten
2 cups (220g) **all-purpose flour**
1 Tbsp **baking powder**
¼ cup (30g) **cocoa powder**
2 Tbsp **unsweetened pear juice**
1 tsp **vanilla extract**
1lb (500g) **ripe pears,** peeled,
  cored and finely chopped

For the icing:
2oz (60g) **unsweetened baking
  chocolate**
1 Tbsp (15g) **unsalted butter**
½ cup (60g) **confectioners sugar**
Approx. 2 Tbsp **whole milk**

Preheat the oven to 300°F/150°C.
Grease and line a deep 8-in (20-cm)
round cake pan.

In a mixing bowl, cream together the
butter and dark sugar until pale in
color and creamy in texture. Gradually
whisk in the eggs with 4 Tbsp flour.
Sift in the remaining flour together with
the baking powder and cocoa; fold in
carefully together with the pear juice,
vanilla extract and chopped pears.

Pile the mixture into the prepared pan
and smooth the top. Bake in the oven
for 1 to 1¼ hours until risen and
golden, and a skewer inserted into the
center comes out clean. Leave to cool
in pan for 10 minutes before turning
onto a wire rack to cook completely.
Wrap in foil and store for 24 hours.

For the icing, put the chocolate and
butter in a saucepan and melt over
gentle heat. Transfer to a heatproof
bowl and sift in the sugar. Gradually
whisk together, adding sufficient milk
to form a smooth, spreadable
consistency. Spread over the pear
cake to serve.

Smoked chicken and pear salad

Light lunch

You can prepare this salad a few hours in advance, as the lemon juice will prevent the pears from browning. The salad makes an excellent starter, and its combination of flavors will certainly tempt the taste buds.

Serves 4

4 ripe pears
Juice of ½ lemon
1 radicchio lettuce
1 small head Cos lettuce
12oz (350g) skinless smoked
    chicken, sliced

For the dressing:
4oz (125g) crumbly blue cheese, e.g.
    Stilton, Roquefort or Danish Blue
½ cup (60g) walnut pieces
4 Tbsp mayonnaise
2 Tbsp white wine vinegar
1 Tbsp walnut oil
Freshly ground black pepper

Peel and core the pears. Cut each into six equal pieces and brush with lemon juice. Set aside. Break up the lettuce leaves, rinse and shake dry.

Arrange the lettuce on four serving plates and top with pear and smoked chicken pieces. Cover and chill until required.

For the dressing, place all the ingredients in a blender or food processor and blend for a few seconds until smooth and creamy. Serve the dressing spooned over the salad.

Smoked chicken and pear salad

Spiced red cabbage with quince

Spiced red cabbage with quince

Tangy

This interesting combination is the perfect side dish to accompany richer meats such as pheasant, duck or pork. I also love it with sausages and mashed potatoes!

Serves 4 to 6

¼ stick (30g) **unsalted butter**
1 **medium onion,** peeled
  and chopped
1 **bay leaf**
1 **small cinnamon stick,** broken
¼ tsp **ground nutmeg**
⅓ cup (60g) **golden raisins**
1lb (500g) **red cabbage,** trimmed
  and shredded
8oz (250g) **quince,** peeled, cored
  and thinly sliced
4 Tbsp **Raspberry vinegar**
  (see page 155)
½ cup (60g) **light brown sugar**
½ tsp **salt**
Freshly ground black pepper

Melt the butter in a large saucepan and gently fry the onion with the bay leaf and spices for 5 minutes until softened but not browned.

Stir in the raisins, cabbage and quince to coat thoroughly in the onion mixture. Add the remaining ingredients and mix well. Bring to a boil, cover and simmer gently for 40 minutes until tender. Discard the cinnamon and bay leaf before serving.

Fruit with stones

In the mid-to-late summer, peaches, nectarines, plums and apricots are at their best. I think that a peach, as long as it's perfectly ripe, is best eaten just as it is; the skin downy and soft, the flesh tender and sweet, and so juicy that it drips down your chin with every bite! I have used fresh peaches and nectarines in a trifle and a hearty salad, both perfect for summer entertaining.

Apricots and plums, to me, are reminiscent of later summer weeks, almost early autumn, when the days are warm, but there is a slight nip in the air come sundown. For this reason I like to cook these fruits with subtle herbs and spices, to enhance their comforting appeal. The Plum and prune strudel (see page 39) and Upside-down fruit pie (see page 47) are personal favorites.

I've also included cherries in this chapter. Gloriously shiny red and beautiful to look at, they are delicious fresh or cooked, and will always be admired when served up for pudding – try the Fresh cherry compôte (see page 44) or Sugared cherry and lemon cake (see page 45) to see what I mean!

Peach melba trifle

Family favorite

If you are in a hurry, you can use ready-made custard, but for a special occasion, it is worth making your own.

Serves 6–8

1 quantity **Custard sauce** (see page 145)
4 **ripe peaches**
¾ cup (200g) **raspberries**, defrosted if frozen
2 Tbsp **confectioners sugar**
6 x ½-in (1-cm) thick slices **pound cake,** lemon-flavored if possible
6 Tbsp **dessert wine or unsweetened peach juice**
1¼ cups (300ml) **whipping cream**
½ tsp **vanilla extract**

Make up the custard sauce as directed on page 145. Cover the surface with a layer of wax paper and set aside to cool.

Meanwhile, wash and pat dry the peaches. Cut in half and remove the stones, then cut the flesh into thin slices. Wash and pat dry the raspberries if you are using fresh ones, then press through a nylon sieve over a small bowl to remove the seeds and purée the fruit. Sift the confectioners sugar into the fruit and carefully whisk in to sweeten.

Arrange three slices of cake in the bottom of a glass serving bowl and sprinkle over half the wine or juice. Top with one-third of the peach slices and drizzle over half the raspberry purée. Place the remaining cake slices on top and soak in the remaining wine or juice. Top with half the remaining peach slices and the rest of the raspberry purée. Cover and chill for 1 hour to allow the flavors to develop. Cover and chill the remaining peach slices until required.

When you are ready to assemble the trifle, whip the cream with the vanilla extract until soft peaks form. Spoon the custard on top of the cake and fruit, and then spoon over the cream. Cover and chill for an hour before serving. Decorate with the reserved peach slices to serve.

Peach melba trifle

Marbled apricot fool
Vanilla-scented

A very simple combination of ingredients, which presents the flavor of fresh apricots at their best. If you prefer an airier texture, add two whisked egg whites to the apricot custard. Use good-quality ready-made custard to save time. This is also good made with plums.

Serves 6

¼ cup (60g) **extra-fine sugar**
1 cup (250ml) **water**
1lb (500g) **fresh apricots**
1 **vanilla pod**, split down the center
½ **quantity Custard sauce**
   (see page 145)
¼ cup (150ml) **whipping cream**

To serve:
¼ cup (15g) **flaked almonds**, toasted
Wafer-thin ginger crisps
   (see page 157)

Place the sugar in a saucepan and pour over the water. Heat gently, stirring, until the sugar dissolves. Bring to a boil and simmer for 5 minutes.

Meanwhile, halve the apricots and remove the stones. Cut in half again. Add to the saucepan and carefully stir through the sugar syrup to coat all the fruit. Bring back to a boil and simmer very gently for about 15 minutes, stirring occasionally, until just tender. Add the vanilla pod and set aside to cool.

Make up the custard sauce as directed on page 145. Cover the surface with a layer of greaseproof paper and set aside to cool.

Once the apricots are cold, discard the vanilla pod and place the fruit in a blender or food processor (push through a nylon sieve for a smooth texture if preferred). Blend for a few seconds until smooth. Transfer half of the purée to a bowl and set aside. Mix the custard sauce into the remainder of the apricot purée.

Whip the cream until soft peaks form and fold into the custard. Spoon the apricot custard into six serving glasses, adding a little of the reserved purée to the mixture occasionally, marbling the two mixtures together to give a rippled effect. Cover and chill for 1 hour before serving. Serve sprinkled with toasted, flaked almonds and accompany with Wafer-thin ginger crisps (see page 157).

Plum and prune strudel

Buttery and crisp

This recipe has a wintry, even Christmassy, feel to it. I love the combination of fresh and dried fruit flavors, which gives added intensity. The breadcrumb layer helps to soak up the cooking juices and prevent sogginess. This is best served as close to baking as possible.

Serves 8

Generous ½ cup (60g) **fresh white breadcrumbs**
¼ cup (1oz) **pine nuts,** toasted
1½lb (750g) **ripe plums,** halved, stoned and chopped
¾ cup (125g) **light brown sugar**
1 tsp **ground cinnamon**
½ tsp **finely grated orange rind**
2 Tbsp **freshly squeezed orange juice**
¾ cup (125g) **no-soak stoned prunes,** chopped
8 **large sheets filo pastry**
¾ stick (90g) **unsalted butter,** melted
2 Tbsp **confectioners sugar**

To serve:
Light cream

Preheat the oven to 400°F/200°C. Line a large baking sheet with baking parchment.

In one bowl, mix the breadcrumbs and pine nuts together, and in another, put the plums, sugar, cinnamon, orange rind, juice and prunes and mix well. Lay out four sheets of pastry on a work surface, overlapping as necessary to form a rectangle about 20 x 14in (52 x 36cm). Brush well with melted butter to secure together. Repeat with the rest of the pastry and brush all over with butter.

Sprinkle the breadcrumb mixture down the center to within 1in (2.5cm) of either end. Spread the plum mixture evenly on top. Fold over the top and bottom pastry edge on top of the filling, buttering to seal. Fold the pastry over from the long sides to cover the filling completely, and brush with butter to seal. Transfer to the prepared baking sheet and brush with the remaining melted butter.

Bake in the oven for about 40 minutes until crisp and golden. Serve hot, dusted with confectioners sugar and accompanied by light cream.

Baked apricots with bay leaves

Fragrant

I first ate fruit flavored with bay leaves in Cyprus, and enjoyed the refreshing, delicate herbal combination very much. I prefer to eat this dish at room temperature for a fuller flavor. If fresh bay leaves are unavailable, use two dried leaves instead. This recipe also works well with plums.

Serves 6

1½lb (750g) **fresh apricots**
1¼ cup (300ml) **fruity red wine or unsweetened cranberry juice**
½ cup (60g) **light brown sugar**
4 **fresh bay leaves**

To serve:
¼ cup (30g) **pecan halves,** toasted and roughly chopped
Plain yogurt or light cream

Preheat the oven to 350°F/180°C. Wash the apricots and pat dry. Cut in half and remove the stones. Arrange the apricots neatly, cut-side up, in a shallow baking dish.

Pour over the red wine or juice and sprinkle the sugar over the fruit. Push the bay leaves in between the fruit and bake in the oven for about 1 hour until the fruit is tender and a rich red color. Using a slotted spoon, remove the fruit from the juices and place in a heatproof dish.

Strain the cooking juices into a saucepan and bring to a boil. Cook for about 5 minutes until reduced and syrupy. Pour over the fruit and set aside to cool. Cover and chill for 2 hours before serving. To serve, sprinkle over the pecan nuts and serve with plain yogurt or light cream.

Baked apricots with bay leaves

Sweet cherry marzipan bread

Almondy

A lovely teatime treat, served warm and cut into chunks. Delicious served with cherry jam for extra sweetness.

Serves 12

1 cup (250ml) **whole milk**
1 **pinch saffron**
4 cups (500g) **white bread flour**
1½ tsp **salt**
1½ tsp **instant or fast-acting yeast**
8oz (250g) **ready-made marzipan,** finely chopped
2 **eggs,** beaten
1½ cups (250g) **fresh cherries,** stoned and halved
1 Tbsp **confectioners sugar** (optional)

Preheat the oven to 400°F/200°C. Pour the milk into a saucepan and add the saffron. Heat gently until warm but not hot. Set aside to cool for 10 minutes.

Sift the flour and salt into a bowl and stir in the yeast and half the marzipan. Make a well in the center and stir in half of the egg along with the saffron milk. Bring together to form a dough.

Turn the dough out onto a lightly floured surface and knead until smooth. Lightly dust the mixing bowl with flour and replace the dough inside. Cover loosely and leave in a warm place for about 1 hour until doubled in size.

Re-knead the dough and place it on a large baking sheet lined with baking parchment. Press the dough into a round about 10in (25cm) diameter. Brush all over with beaten egg then sprinkle the cherries evenly over the top and gently press into the dough. Cover loosely and set aside for about 40 minutes or until well risen.

Sprinkle with the remaining marzipan and bake in the oven for about 30 minutes until the marzipan is golden and the cherries are tender. Leave to cool on the baking tray. Best served warm and dusted with confectioners sugar, if liked.

Sweet cherry marzipan bread

Fresh cherry compôte

Juicy

Stoning fresh cherries can be a bit of a task, so it's well worth investing in a cherry stoner to help you. This recipe is definitely worth the effort, and all you need to accompany it is some sour cream or crème fraîche.

Serves 4

Scant ¾ cup (150g) **extra-fine sugar**
Scant 1 cup (200ml) **fruity red wine
   or unsweetened orange juice**
Pared rind of 1 **small orange**
2 **star anise**
3 cups (500g) **fresh cherries,
   washed and stoned**

To serve:
Sour cream or crème fraîche
Shortbread fingers (see page 157)

Put the sugar in a saucepan with the wine or orange juice, orange rind and star anise. Heat gently, stirring until dissolved.

Bring to a boil and add the cherries. Simmer gently for about 5 minutes, stirring occasionally, until tender. Remove from the heat and allow to cool completely. Discard the orange rind and star anise.

Transfer to a serving dish, cover and chill for 2 hours before serving with sour cream or crème fraîche. Accompany with Shortbread fingers (see page 157).

Sugared cherry and lemon cake
Crunchy-topped

A moist, close-textured cake guaranteed to be popular with those of us with a sweet tooth, either as a cake or a pudding. If you can leave it alone, the cake will have more flavor if wrapped and stored for a day before serving.

Serves 12

2 sticks (200g) **unsalted butter,**
   softened
1¼ cups (200g) **light brown sugar**
Scant 1 cup (100g) **self-rising flour**
4 **eggs,** beaten
1 pinch **salt**
¾ cup (125g) **ground almonds**
1 tsp **finely grated lemon rind**
Few drops **almond extract**
3 cups (500g) **fresh cherries,** stoned

For the topping:
4 Tbsp **lemon juice**
1 cup (200g) **extra-fine sugar**
¼ cup (45g) **sugar cubes,**
   roughly crushed

To serve:
Light cream (optional)

Preheat the oven to 350°F/180°C. Grease and line a 9-in (22-cm) springform cake pan.

In a mixing bowl, beat together the butter and sugar until pale and creamy.

Gradually whisk in half the flour with the eggs, then sift in the remainder with the salt. Add the ground almonds, lemon rind and almond extract and fold in carefully until well combined. Fold in half the cherries.

Pile the mixture into the prepared pan and smooth the top. Drop the remaining cherries over the top and push them in lightly. Bake in the center of the oven for about 1 hour until golden and firm in the center. Leave to cool in the pan, setting on a wire rack.

While the cake is baking, prepare the topping. Mix the lemon juice and extra-fine sugar together and spoon over the cake as soon as it comes out of the oven. Sprinkle with the sugar pieces and leave to cool completely. Release from the pan, wrap and store for 1 day before slicing and serving with light cream if liked.

Upside-down fruit pie

Upside-down fruit pie
French-style

Traditionally made with apples, this French-style tart works very well with stoned fruit. A little bit of spice adds extra flavor, but you can omit it if you prefer.

Serves 6

1lb 3½oz (600g) **plums or apricots**
Generous ½ cup (125g) **extra-fine sugar**
¼ tsp **ground nutmeg**
8oz (250g) **puff pastry,** defrosted if frozen

To serve:
Vanilla ice cream

Preheat the oven to 400°F/200°C. Loosely line a 9-in (23-cm) round shallow cake pan with a piece of baking parchment.

Halve the plums or apricots, prize out the stones and set aside.

Sprinkle the sugar evenly over the base of a heavy-based saucepan and heat until it begins to melt, tilting the pan to cook evenly and making sure all the sugar is used. Once the sugar is lightly caramelized and a liquid, drizzle it over the base of the pan before it begins to set. Dust the caramel lightly with nutmeg.

Starting from the center, arrange the fruit halves to fit snugly over the base of the pan, leaving a slight gap around the edge of the pan.

Roll the pastry out on a lightly floured surface to a square about 10in (25cm). Place the pastry on top of the fruit and tuck the pastry edges down between the fruit and the paper. Cook in the oven for 35–40 minutes until puffed up, crisp and lightly golden. Cool for 10 minutes, then invert onto a warm serving plate and peel away the paper. Serve warm with vanilla ice cream.

Greek-style feta and nectarine salad

Greek-style feta and nectarine salad

Mediterranean

When nectarines are at their most juicy and ripe, this is an ideal way to serve them, as their sweetness complements the slightly acidic feta cheese.

Serves 4

1 green pepper
2 ripe nectarines
¼ cucumber
1 small red onion
1 Cos lettuce
Generous ¼ cup (90g) **Greek black olives**, stoned
7oz (200g) **block feta cheese**
6 Tbsp **plain yogurt**
2 Tbsp **white wine vinegar**
4 Tbsp **chopped mint**
1 Tbsp **extra-fine sugar**
Salt and freshly ground black pepper

To serve:
Pita bread

Wash, halve and deseed the pepper. Cut into bite-sized chunks and place in a serving bowl. Wash and pat dry the nectarines. Cut in half and prize out the stone, cut each half into four wedges, then mix carefully with the pepper.

Wash and pat dry the cucumber and cut into small chunks. Peel the onion and cut into thin slices. Discard any damaged outer leaves from the lettuce; wash and shake dry, then tear the leaves into small pieces. Mix everything together in the serving bowl along with the olives.

Cut the feta cheese into cubes and toss into the salad. Cover and chill for at least 1 hour before serving.

Mix the remaining ingredients together in a small bowl, cover and chill until required. Serve the salad with the yogurt mixture as a dressing, accompanied by warm pita bread.

Mackerel with sweet and sour plum relish

Mackerel with sweet and sour plum relish

Tangy

As we all know, oily fish is very good for us, although it can be difficult to think of interesting ways to serve it. This combination of sweet fruit in a sour dressing complements the richness of the fish, and I'm sure it will become a favorite.

Serves 4

4 tsp **wholegrain mustard**
2 Tbsp **honey**
8 x 3½-oz (100-g) **mackerel fillets**
2 Tbsp **balsamic vinegar**
2 tsp **sesame oil**
Salt and freshly ground black pepper
8oz (250g) **ripe plums,** halved, stoned and finely chopped
1 **medium red or yellow pepper,** deseeded and finely chopped
4 **green onions,** trimmed and finely chopped
1 **medium carrot,** peeled and grated
60g (2oz) **bean sprouts,** roughly chopped

To serve:
Crusty bread

Mix together the mustard and 1 Tbsp honey. Wash and pat dry the mackerel fillets and season on both sides.

Preheat the grill to medium. Arrange the mackerel fillets on the grill rack, flesh-side up, and brush with the mustard and honey. Cook for 5 to 6 minutes, without turning, until tender and cooked through. Drain and set aside while you prepare the relish.

Mix the remaining honey with the vinegar and sesame oil and season well. Place the remaining ingredients in a bowl and mix in the vinegar and oil dressing.

While the mackerel is still warm, flake it from the skin. Arrange the relish on serving plates and top with the mackerel. Serve with crusty bread.

Berries and soft fruit

I am fortunate enough to live in an area of Scotland where soft fruits grow very well, enabling me to enjoy the best locally grown produce. The strawberry season (weather permitting) is from mid May onwards, with raspberries a few weeks later. Wild blueberries ripen on the scrubland, and in mid-to-late summer blackberries (or brambles, as they are known in Scotland) ripen in the hedgerows. All provide a bright, jeweled feast on my doorstep.

You'll find plenty of ideas to incorporate these juicy little wonders in sweet and savory dishes. I have used subtle seasonings in these recipes so that you can appreciate the delicate, often perfumed, flavors of the fruits themselves. Particularly good is the traditional Blackberry and apple cobbler (see page 59) – a family favorite – and the Berry pavlova (see page 71), simply bursting with flavor and color.

You'll also find recipes using rhubarb, a stalwart of some of our classic puddings. Together with rhubarb there is another familiar fruit, the cranberry – here you'll find that there is more to the cranberry than just sauce-making.

Poached rhubarb with ginger cake

Zingy

This is a winning combination of flavors, and the cake is best made the day before for a tastier result. If you haven't time to make your own ginger cake, then use a ready-made ginger cake.

Serves 4

For the ginger cake:
¼ cup (60g) **molasses**
¼ cup (60g) **corn syrup**
Scant ½ cup 60g (2oz) **dark brown sugar**
½ stick 60g (2oz) **unsalted butter**
Generous ¼ cup (75ml) **whole milk**
1 cup (125g) **self-rising flour**
¼ tsp **salt**
½ tsp **ground ginger**
½ tsp **ground cinnamon**
1oz (30g) **preserved ginger, finely chopped**

For the rhubarb:
12oz (350g) **rhubarb**
Generous ½ cup (125g) **extra-fine sugar**
½ cup (125ml) **freshly squeezed orange juice**

Preheat the oven to 325°F/170°C. Grease and line a 2¼-cup (500-g) loaf pan.

Place the molasses, syrup, sugar, butter and milk in a saucepan, and heat gently, stirring, until melted together. Sift the flour, salt and spices in a bowl, and make a well in the center. Add the ginger and gradually stir in the melted ingredients until well mixed. Transfer to the prepared pan and bake in the center of the oven for about 55 minutes until risen and firm to the touch. Leave to cool in the pan, then remove from the pan, wrap in wax paper and then foil, and store for 24 hours.

Trim and cut the rhubarb into 4-in (10-cm) lengths. Place the sugar in a medium frying pan with a lid and pour in the orange juice. Heat gently, stirring until dissolved, then bring to a boil and simmer for 3 minutes.

Add the rhubarb to the pan, laying the pieces side by side. Bring back to a boil, cover and simmer for 3 minutes. Carefully turn the rhubarb over, cover and cook for a further 3–4 minutes until just cooked. Remove from the heat and allow to cool completely. Transfer to a serving dish, cover and chill for 2 hours before serving.

To serve, slice the cake into 8 pieces. Place two slices on each serving plate and spoon over rhubarb and juices.

Poached rhubarb with ginger cake

Rhubarb and raspberry crumble

Favorite

This comforting pudding is best served hot with Custard sauce (see page 145). You can replace the raspberries with small whole strawberries if preferred.

Serves 4 to 6

1lb (500g) **rhubarb**
⅔ cup (150g) **fresh raspberries**
Generous ½ cup (125g) **extra-fine sugar**
1½ cups (180g) **self-rising flour**
1 stick (125g) **butter**
½ cup (60g) **ground almonds**

To serve:
Custard sauce (see page 145)

Preheat the oven to 400°F/200°C. Trim the rhubarb and cut into 2-in (5-cm) lengths. Place half the rhubarb in the bottom of a 5-cup (1.2-L) oval baking dish.

Top with the raspberries and scant ¼ cup (30g) sugar, then the remaining rhubarb and another scant 1 cup (30g) sugar. Set aside.

Sift the flour into a bowl and rub in the butter until well combined and the mixture starts to cling together in lumps. Stir in the remaining sugar and the ground almonds.

Set the rhubarb dish on a baking sheet, and carefully sprinkle the crumble topping evenly over the fruit. Bake in the oven for about 45 minutes covering the top with foil if it browns too quickly. Pierce the rhubarb in the center of the dish to make sure it is tender. Best served hot, with Custard sauce (see page 145).

Fruity spiced cranberry tea loaf

Sweet treat

You can use whatever dried fruit you like in this recipe – just keep the pieces small. Tea loaves are moist and keep for up to a week if they are wrapped well and stored in an airtight container.

Makes 10 slices

Scant 1 cup (150g) **golden raisins**
Scant 1 cup (150g) **dried apricots,**
  chopped
1 cup (125g) **fresh cranberries**
1 cup (150g) **light brown sugar**
Scant ½ cup (100ml) **cold black tea**
Scant ½ cup (100ml) **unsweetened**
  cranberry juice
1 **egg, beaten**
2 cups (250g) **self-rising flour**
1 pinch **salt**
2 tsp **pumpkin pie spice**

Place the raisins, apricots and cranberries in a bowl together with the sugar and pour over the tea and cranberry juice. Cover and set in a cool place for about 4 hours, stirring occasionally, until the dried fruit has plumped up.

Preheat the oven to 350°F/150°C. Grease and line a 4½-cup (1-kg) loaf pan.

Mix the egg into the soaked fruit. Sift the flour, salt and spice over the fruit and carefully fold in until well incorporated and the mixture forms a thick, fruity batter.

Pour into the prepared pan and bake in the oven for about 1½ hours until golden and risen, and a skewer inserted into the center comes out clean. Transfer to a wire rack to cool. Slice thinly to serve and spread with butter or cream cheese.

Blackberry and apple cobbler

Blackberry and apple cobbler

Traditional

An old-fashioned fruit pudding with a soft scone topping. It works well with most berry fruits, but blackberries are a personal favorite.

Serves 4

2 eating apples
Juice of 1 lemon
1¼ cups (350g) **fresh blackberries,**
   washed and hulled
¼ cup (60g) **extra-fine sugar**

For the topping:
2 cups (250g) **self-raising flour**
1 tsp **pumpkin pie spice**
1¼ sticks (150g) **unsalted butter**
¼ cup (60g) **extra-fine sugar**
Approx. ½ cup (90ml) **milk**
2 Tbsp **granulated sugar**

To serve:
Light cream or Custard sauce (see
   page 145)

Preheat the oven to 375°F/190°C. Peel and core the apples and cut into small chunks. Place in a bowl and toss in the lemon juice. Stir in the blackberries and sugar. Spoon into the bottom of a 5-cup (1.2-L) oval baking dish. Cover with foil and place in the oven for 15 minutes.

Meanwhile, make the topping. Sift the flour and spice into a mixing bowl. Rub 1 stick (125g) butter into the flour and stir in the extra-fine sugar. Stir in enough milk to form a soft dough.

Turn onto a lightly floured surface and knead gently. Press or roll out to a thickness of about ½in (1cm). Using a 2-in (5-cm) round cutter, stamp out 16 circles, re-rolling the dough as necessary.

Place the rounds, overlapping, on top of the dish. Melt the remaining butter and brush it over the top. Sprinkle with granulated sugar and place on a baking sheet. Bake for 25–30 minutes until risen and golden. Serve warm with light cream or Custard sauce (see page 145).

Soft-bake blueberry and white chocolate cookies

Tempting

Half cookie, half cake. Once you've baked these you'll not be able to leave them alone, but, if you can resist, they do freeze well!

Makes 30

1½ sticks (180g) **unsalted butter, softened**
Scant 1 cup (150g) **light brown sugar**
1 **egg yolk**
2 cups (250g) **all-purpose flour**
1 **pinch salt**
½ tsp **baking powder**
1 tsp **vanilla extract**
4oz (125g) **white chocolate,** cut into small chunks
⅔ cup (150g) **fresh blueberries**

Preheat the oven to 375°F/190°C. Line two large baking sheets with baking parchment.

In a mixing bowl, beat together the butter and sugar until light and creamy. Beat in the egg yolk and carefully stir in the flour, salt, baking powder, vanilla extract, chocolate chunks and blueberries to make a firm dough.

Form into walnut-sized balls and place, a little apart, on the prepared baking sheets, then press down gently to flatten the tops. Bake in the oven for about 12 minutes until just firm and lightly browned. Cool for 10 minutes on the baking sheets, then transfer to wire racks to cool further. Even more delicious served slightly warm with ice cream!

Soft-bake blueberry and white chocolate cookies

Blueberry cheese ice cream

Indulgent

A lovely lilac-colored dessert, perfect for cooling you down on a summer's day. This is a rich, fondant-style ice cream that doesn't need stirring during freezing. The mixture won't freeze solidly because of the sugar syrup, but still needs to soften slightly before serving.

Serves 4 to 6

1 cup (200g) **extra-fine sugar**
1½ cups (350ml) **water**
¾ cup (200g) **fresh blueberries**
1 **vanilla pod,** split down the center
1¾ cups (400g) **full-fat cream cheese**
⅔ cup (150ml) **heavy cream**

To serve:
Soft-bake blueberry and white
   chocolate cookies (see page 60)

Put the sugar in a saucepan with the water and heat, stirring, until dissolved. Bring to a boil then simmer, uncovered, for 10 minutes until syrupy. Remove from the heat and stir in the blueberries and vanilla pod. Allow to cool completely.

Discard the vanilla pod, transfer the blueberry syrup to a blender or food processor and blend for a few seconds until smooth.

In a mixing bowl, gradually whisk the blueberry syrup into the cream cheese. Lightly whip the cream and fold into the mixture.

Transfer to a freezer container, cover and place in the coldest part of the freezer and freeze for at least 4 hours until firmly frozen. Stand at room temperature for about 15 minutes to soften before serving. Accompany with Soft-bake blueberry and white chocolate cookies (see page 60).

Warm duck, mushroom and blackberry salad

Autumnal

This makes an impressive starter, and if wild mushrooms are in season (and affordable), then choose them above cultivated varieties, as their flavor takes a lot of beating. Serve simply with crusty whole-wheat bread.

Serves 4

2 x 8-oz (250-g) **boneless duck breasts**
Salt and freshly ground black pepper
1 pinch **nutmeg**
1 **shallot,** peeled and finely chopped
1 **clove garlic,** peeled and finely chopped
½ cup (125g) **fresh blackberries,** washed and hulled
4½ cups (350g) **assorted mushrooms,** wiped and sliced
2 Tbsp **walnut oil**
2 tsp **honey**
3 Tbsp **Blackberry vinegar** (see page 155)
1 bunch **watercress,** trimmed and washed

Wash and pat dry the duck breasts and season on both sides with salt, pepper and a little nutmeg. Heat a heavy-based frying pan until very hot, press the duck breasts into the pan, skin side down, and fry for 2 minutes until richly golden. Drain the fat into another frying pan; turn the duck over, reduce the heat and cook gently for 20 minutes. Turn the duck and continue to cook for a further 10–15 minutes or until cooked to your liking.

Meanwhile, heat the reserved duck fat and gently fry the shallot and garlic for 5 minutes until softened but not browned. Stir in the blackberries and mushrooms and cook, stirring, for about 2 minutes, until just wilting – taking care not to overcook the mushrooms. Remove from the heat and gently stir in the walnut oil, honey and vinegar. Season and set aside.

When the duck is ready, slice the breasts thinly. Divide the watercress between four serving plates and, using a slotted spoon, top with the mushroom mixture. Add a few slices of duck and spoon over the mushroom cooking juices. Serve while still warm.

Strawberry granita

Rose pink

This Italian water ice is very refreshing and is often served in between courses as a palate cleanser. I like the Middle Eastern flavor of rosewater, but if the flavor of the strawberries you are using is perfumed, then it may be unnecessary.

Serves 4 to 6

Generous ½ cup (125g) **extra-fine sugar**
2 cups (475ml) **water**
3¾ cups (500g) **strawberries**
2 tsp **rosewater (optional)**
Rose geranium leaves and rose petals, to decorate

Place the sugar in a saucepan with the water. Heat, stirring, until the sugar dissolves, then bring to a boil and simmer for 5 minutes.

Meanwhile, wash and hull the strawberries, then cut in half. Add to the syrup and simmer for a further 5 minutes until the strawberries are soft. Remove from the heat and set aside to cool for 30 minutes, then push through a nylon sieve, and allow to cool completely.

Stir in the rosewater, if using. Pour the cold strawberry syrup into a freezer-proof container and place in the coldest part of your freezer. The syrup will begin to freeze after about 2½ hours, and at this stage, you need to beat the ice crystals to break them up. Return to the freezer and stir every 30–40 minutes until the crystals form evenly and start to cling together. Store in the least cool part of your freezer until ready to serve.

To serve, beat the granita to break up any clumps of ice crystals and spoon into serving glasses. Decorate with the leaves and petals, and serve immediately.

Easy summer pudding

Luscious

The traditional recipe for this dessert calls for it to be left with a weight on it for 24 hours, but this is a quicker version, which offers the same flavors in a fraction of the time.

Serves 4

⅔ cup (180g) **raspberries**
⅔ cup (180g) **blackberries**
½ cup (125g) **strawberries**
½ cup (90g) **extra-fine sugar**
1 **vanilla pod, split down the center**
4 x ½-in (1-cm) **thick slices brioche-type loaf**

To serve:
Plain yogurt

Prepare the berries and place in a saucepan. Add the sugar and 3 Tbsp water. Bring to a boil, cover and simmer gently for about 5 minutes until the fruit just begins to soften. Remove from the heat add the vanilla pod and set aside to cool. When cool, discard the vanilla pod.

Slice the crusts from the bread and cut in quarters. Place a piece of bread in the bottom of four serving glasses or tumblers and spoon over a little fruit. Continue layering with bread and fruit, finishing with fruit. Cover and chill for 30 minutes. Serve with a dollop of plain yogurt on top.

Raspberry cheesecake

Raspberry cheesecake

Decadent

This is one of the easiest cheesecakes I've ever made, as it involves no gelatin or eggs. The texture is dense and cloying, and the fresh flavor of the raspberries is ideal to counteract the richness.

Serves 10

12oz (350g) **double chocolate chip cookies,** crushed
1 stick (125g) **unsalted butter**
8oz (250g) **white chocolate,** broken into pieces
1¼ cup (300g) **full-fat cream cheese,** at room temperature
1 cup (250ml) **heavy cream,** at room temperature
1 tsp **vanilla extract**
Scant 1 cup (250g) **fresh raspberries plus extra to decorate (optional)**

Grease and line the base of a deep 9-in (22-cm) springform cake pan. Place the cookies in a bowl. Melt the butter, pour over the cookies and bind together. Press onto the base of the pan using the back of a metal spoon. Chill until required.

Place the chocolate pieces in a heatproof bowl and melt over a pan of barely simmering water. Set aside for 10 minutes until it is cooled, but still warm. In a large mixing bowl, whisk together the cream cheese, double cream and vanilla extract.

Fold in the warm white chocolate and raspberries and spoon the mixture over the cookie base. Smooth the top and chill for 2–3 hours until set. Note: if the chocolate is too cool, it will not mix in properly and will make the cheese filling lumpy.

To serve, release the cheesecake from the pan and place on a serving plate. Top with extra raspberries if liked.

Raspberry and orange terrine

Fresh

This looks stunning, full of flavor and color. It is a good dessert to serve after a filling main course, or for those watching their weight.

Serves 6

4½ cups (560g) **frozen raspberries**
3 Tbsp **extra-fine sugar**
3 Tbsp **boiling water**
⅔ cup (150ml) **hot water**
4 level tsp **Knox gelatin**
2 cups (450ml) **freshly squeezed orange juice**
3 Tbsp **orange liqueur (optional)**
Mint sprigs, raspberries and orange zest, to decorate

To serve:
Light cream or plain yogurt

Place the frozen raspberries in a 4½-cup (1-kg) loaf pan and return to the freezer until required. Dissolve the sugar in the boiling water and allow to cool. Pour the very hot water into a heatproof bowl and sprinkle over the gelatin. Stir until dissolved and then set aside to cool for 30 minutes.

Stir the sugared water and gelatin mixture into the orange juice along with the liqueur, if using. Pour over the raspberries in the pan, pushing the raspberries down into the gelatin for about 3 minutes to make sure they are completely covered and set in position. Chill in the fridge for at least 2 hours until set.

To serve, dip the loaf pan in hot water for a few seconds to loosen and invert the terrine onto a serving platter. Decorate with mint sprigs, raspberries and orange zest, and serve sliced with light cream or plain yogurt.

Raspberry and orange terrine

Berry pavlova

Berry pavlova

Marshmallowy

Another favorite combination of mine is meringue and cream. When berries are in season, this is a simple and effective way to enjoy them, and the lemon syrup really enhances their flavor.

Serves 8

4 large **egg whites**
1 pinch **salt**
½ tsp **cream of tartar**
2 cups (400g) **extra-fine sugar**
1 tsp **Raspberry vinegar**
   (see page 155)
Few drops **vanilla extract**
Juice and finely grated rind of
   2 **lemons**
1¼ cups (300ml) **whipping cream**
1¼ cups (300g) **assorted prepared**
   fresh berries: blueberries,
   strawberries, blackberries and
   raspberries

Preheat the oven to 275°F/140°C. Line a large baking sheet with baking parchment and draw a 10-in (24-cm) circle on the paper.

In a large, grease-free bowl, whisk the egg whites with the salt and cream of tartar, until stiff and dry. Gradually whisk in ¾ cup (150g) of the sugar, and then carefully fold in a further ¾ cup (150g) sugar, together with the vinegar and vanilla extract, to form a thick, glossy meringue.

Pile the meringue onto the baking sheet, keeping within the marked circle, smoothing and scooping the meringue from the sides back on top to make a thick "cake." Bake in the oven, on the bottom shelf, for about 1½ hours, until pale cream in color, crisp on the outside, yet marshmallowy inside. Turn off the oven and leave to cool – it will probably sink in the middle.

Meanwhile, place the lemon juice and rind in a small saucepan with the remaining sugar and stir over a low heat until dissolved. Bring to a boil and simmer gently for 2–3 minutes until syrupy. Set aside to cool.

When you are ready to serve, place the meringue on a serving plate. Whip the cream until just peaking, and pile on top of the meringue. Sprinkle with the berries and drizzle with lemon syrup. Serve immediately – do not refrigerate, as the meringue will start to dissolve.

Turkey burgers with cranberry relish

Turkey burgers with cranberry relish

Contemporary

You can use all ground turkey if you prefer in this recipe, but the burgers will be less moist. They can be prepared the day before and cooked just before serving, as can the relish.

Serves 4

1lb (500g) **ground turkey**
8oz (250g) **pork sausage**
1 **small onion,** peeled and finely chopped
1 Tbsp **wholegrain mustard**
2 Tbsp **tomato ketchup**
1 **small bunch thyme**
4 Tbsp **dry white breadcrumbs**
Salt and freshly ground black pepper
2 Tbsp **sunflower oil**

For the relish:
1 **small red onion,** peeled and thinly sliced
½ cup (125g) **cranberries**
Scant ½ cup (100ml) **cloudy apple juice**
1 **eating apple,** washed, cored and chopped
1 **medium orange,** peeled, segmented and chopped
2 Tbsp **maple syrup**

First make the burgers. Place the ground turkey and sausage in a bowl and mix in the onion. Add the mustard and ketchup. Strip the leaves from the thyme and add them to the mixture together with the breadcrumbs and seasoning. Bring together with your hands.

Divide into eight equal pieces and form each into a rough burger shape about ½in (1cm) thick. Place on a plate lined with baking parchment and chill for 30 minutes.

Meanwhile, make the relish. Place the onion and cranberries in a saucepan and pour over the apple juice. Bring to a boil, cover and simmer for about 5 minutes until the cranberries are just softened. Remove from the heat and allow to cool.

When you are ready to cook the burgers, heat the oil in a large frying pan and gently fry the burgers for 10–12 minutes on each side until golden and cooked through. Drain on paper towel and keep warm.

To finish the relish, gently mix the chopped apple into the cranberries together with the chopped orange segments and maple syrup. Pile into a serving bowl and serve with the burgers.

Smoked salmon, cucumber and strawberry salad

Healthy

This pretty salad makes a deliciously refreshing light meal or a starter to a romantic meal. Its ingredients have delicate flavors, so it is best to serve the salad at room temperature or only slightly chilled. Ideal accompanied with chilled pink champagne or a dry rosé wine.

Serves 4

½ **cucumber**
Scant 1 cup (250g) **small strawberries**
8oz (250g) **smoked salmon**
4oz (125g) **tiger shrimp**, peeled
2 Tbsp **Raspberry vinegar** (see page 155)
2 Tbsp **light olive oil**
2 tsp **honey**
1 pinch **salt**
Freshly ground pink peppercorns
1 small bunch **basil**

Peel the cucumber if preferred, and then halve lengthways and slice thinly on the diagonal. Place the cucumber slices in a bowl. Wash and hull the strawberries. Halve them and add to the bowl. Toss the ingredients gently together. Set aside.

Slice the smoked salmon into ribbon-like strips. Wash and pat dry the shrimp. Whisk the vinegar, oil and honey together, and season.

To serve, pile the cucumber and strawberries on four serving plates and top each with some smoked salmon and shrimp. Drizzle with dressing, sprinkle with extra ground pink pepper, if liked, and scatter over a few basil leaves.

Smoked salmon, cucumber and strawberry salad

Melon and grapes

Probably the best fruit for cooling you down in a hurry is a perfectly ripe, lightly chilled melon. Nothing beats its thirst-quenching sweet and juicy flesh on a hot day.

All varieties of melon have a very delicate flavor, but each has its own subtleties. Some, like cantaloupe, are more fragrant; the bright red flesh of a watermelon is less sweet and more refreshing; the honeydew has a very sweet, juicy flesh, which makes a deliciously light and healthy snack when you're in need of a sugar hit.

Melons can be served in both a sweet or savory context; choose light flavors such as chicken, shellfish or salad vegetables in order to enjoy the fruit at its best. Try the Chilled melon and cucumber soup (see page 89) or the Asian-style Watermelon and crab salad (see page 90) for something out of the ordinary.

Grapes are just as versatile. As they are often served as part of an after-dinner cheese course, I have used them to finish off a savory Blue cheese cheesecake (see page 85). You can also cook them successfully as well: I have baked them in puff pastry with a rich almond paste – ideal served at teatime.

Grape syllabub

Creamy

This is an old English dessert traditionally made with frothy milk, straight from the cow, poured over wine. There are many versions nowadays, and this one uses grape juice instead of wine.

Serves 6

Finely grated rind and juice of
  1 lemon
¼ cup (60g) **extra-fine sugar**
4 Tbsp **unsweetened white grape juice**
2 cups (180g) **seedless green grapes,** washed and halved
4 **macaroons,** finely chopped
1¼ cups (300ml) **heavy cream**

Place the lemon rind and juice in a small, non-metallic bowl and set aside to soak for 2 hours. Stir in the sugar and grape juice, and cover and chill for 1 hour or until ready to serve.

When you are ready to serve, divide the grapes and macaroons among six wine glasses. Pour the cream into a mixing bowl and begin whisking. As the cream begins to thicken, gradually pour in the lemon and grape juice mixture. Continue whisking until just peaking and then pile into the glasses. Serve immediately.

You can prepare this up to 30 minutes in advance and keep in the fridge. After this time, the juices begin to separate from the cream.

Grape syllabub

Almond and grape pastry

Crumbly

To enjoy this pastry fully, it is best eaten warm – the grapes will be juicier, the almond filling richer and the pastry flakier. Excellent served with strong coffee as a mid-morning treat.

Serves 8

1½ cups (200g) **ground almonds**
Generous ½ cup (125g) **extra-fine sugar**
Seeds from 4 **green cardamom pods,** crushed
1 tsp **good-quality vanilla extract**
2 eggs, beaten
7oz (200g) **puff pastry,** defrosted if frozen
2¼ cups (200g) **small seedless red grapes,** washed
½ cup (60g) **flaked almonds**
1 Tbsp **confectioners sugar**

To serve:
Light cream

Preheat the oven to 400°F/200°C. Line a baking sheet with baking parchment.

Mix together the ground almonds, extra-fine sugar, cardamom and vanilla.

Bind together with one of the eggs to form a thick paste. Set aside.

Roll out the pastry on a lightly floured board to form a rectangle about 14 x 10in (35 x 25cm). Roll or press the almond paste to form a thick strip about 3in (7cm) wide, and position it down the center of the pastry, about 1in (2.5cm) away from either end. Pile the grapes on top, gently pressing them into the almond paste.

Brush the edges of the pastry with beaten egg and fold up the two shorter sides, and then the longer sides to cover the filling completely. Press the top down lightly to seal. Transfer to the baking sheet and brush with more egg. Sprinkle with the almonds and bake in the oven for 35–40 minutes until golden and crisp. Cool on the baking sheet then dust with confectioners sugar before slicing to serve. Best served warm, with light cream.

Almond and grape pastry

Melon and mint tea salad

Melon and mint tea salad

Moroccan-style

I love the refreshing flavors in this salad; you could serve it as a starter or a light dessert. Moroccans drink their tea pretty strong and sweet, so I have made the syrup lighter to complement the melon.

Serves 4

½ quantity **Sugar syrup**
  (see page 144)
1 tsp **tea leaves**
⅔ cup (150ml) **boiling water**
1 **small bunch mint, plus extra**
  to serve
½ **small green-fleshed melon,**
  e.g. Galia
½ **small orange-fleshed melon,**
  e.g. Cantaloupe
¼ **Honeydew melon**

First make the syrup as directed on page 144 and allow to cool. Place the tea leaves in a heatproof measuring cup and pour over the boiling water. Allow to brew for 3 minutes, then strain into another cup and put the small bunch of mint leaves into the tea. Allow to cool.

Scoop the seeds out of the melons. Slice off the skin and chop the flesh into small pieces and place in a serving bowl. Cover and chill until required.

Once the syrup and tea are cold, discard the mint leaves and mix the syrup and tea together. Pour over the melons, mix well, cover and chill for 30 minutes. Mix again before serving, sprinkled with extra mint leaves.

Blue cheese cheesecake

Blue cheese cheesecake

After-dinner

You can serve this dish instead of the usual cheeseboard after a special dinner, or serve slices as part of a buffet or a light lunch with salad. For maximum flavor, use a tangy blue cheese.

Serves 8

6oz (180g) **graham crackers,** crushed
¾ stick (90g) **unsalted butter,** melted
8oz (250g) **strong-flavoured blue cheese,** e.g. mature Stilton, Roquefort or Danish Blue
⅔ cup (150ml) **sour cream**
3 **eggs**
2¼ cup (200g) **black grapes**
Celery leaves, to garnish

Preheat the oven to 350°F/180°C. Grease and line the base and sides of a 8-in (20-cm) round springform cake pan.

Place the crushed crackers in a bowl and mix in the melted butter. Press onto the base of the pan using the back of a spoon and chill until required.

Crumble the blue cheese into a blender or food processor and add the sour cream and eggs. Blend for a few seconds until smooth. Pour over the cracker base. Bake in the center of the oven for about 40 minutes until just set. Leave to cool in the pan. When cool, release from the pan and place on a serving plate. Cover and chill for 2 hours.

To serve, wash the grapes, halve and remove the seeds. Arrange on top of the cheesecake and garnish with celery leaves. Cut into 8 slices to serve.

■ *You can use crushed herb- or cheese-flavored crackers as a base if preferred.*

Chicken Véronique

Retro

I remember my mom cooking this dish for her dinner parties back in the 1970s when French bistro cooking was the trend. It has fallen out of fashion these days, so I think it's high time to revive it.

Serves 4

4 x 5-oz (150-g) **boneless chicken breasts**
Salt and freshly ground black pepper
¼ cup (30g) **all-purpose flour**
¼ stick (30g) **unsalted butter**
2 Tbsp **olive oil**
2 **shallots**, peeled and finely chopped
1 clove **garlic**, peeled and finely chopped
⅔ cup (150ml) **dry white wine**
1¼ cups (300ml) **chicken stock**
1 **bay leaf**
1¼ cups (180g) **seedless green grapes**, washed
2 Tbsp **chopped fresh tarragon**
4 Tbsp **heavy cream**

To serve:
Selection of vegetables
New potatoes or French fries

Wash and pat dry the chicken breasts. Season the flour and rub into the chicken on both sides. In a deep frying pan with a lid, melt the butter with the oil until bubbling and then fry the chicken for about 10 minutes, turning occasionally, until golden all over.

Remove with a slotted spoon or tongs and set aside. Gently fry the shallots and garlic for 5 minutes until softened but not browned, and then gradually stir in the wine and stock. Add the bay leaf and return the chicken to the pan. Bring to a boil, cover and simmer gently for 30 minutes.

Add the grapes, tarragon and cream. Continue to cook for a further 5 minutes until the chicken is tender and cooked through. Discard the bay leaf and serve with a selection of vegetables and boiled new potatoes or French fries.

Melon, shrimp and bacon salad

Contemporary

An updated version of the more traditional and popular shrimp cocktail starter. Use orange- or green-fleshed melon, as you prefer. The salad works equally well with crab or other white fish instead of shrimp.

Serves 4

2 Tbsp **low-fat plain yogurt**
2 Tbsp **mayonnaise**
½ tsp **mild curry powder**
1 **small orange-fleshed melon,**
   e.g. Cantaloupe
12oz (350g) **large peeled shrimp,**
   defrosted if frozen
6 slices **Parma ham**
1 **bunch watercress,** washed
   and trimmed
Freshly ground black pepper
1 **lime,** quartered

Mix together the yogurt, mayonnaise and curry powder in a small bowl. Cover and chill until required.

Quarter the melon and scoop out the seeds. Slice off the skin and chop the flesh roughly; place in a bowl. Wash and pat dry the shrimp and mix into the melon. Set aside.

Heat a frying pan until very hot and lay the slices of Parma ham in the bottom. Cook for a few seconds on each side until crisp and shriveled. Drain well and then chop finely. Toss into the melon and shrimp along with the watercress.

To serve, pile the salad onto serving plates. Top each serving with a dollop of curried mayonnaise and season with black pepper. Serve with wedges of lime to squeeze over.

Chilled melon and cucumber soup

Chilled melon and cucumber soup

Refreshing

An unusual starter ideal for a summer lunch. The flavor and color is delicate, but use fresh stock for best results. It is quite rich, so serve very simply, ladled over ice cubes.

Serves 4 to 6

1 large cucumber, weighing
  approx. 15oz (450g)
2½ cups (600ml) good-quality
  chicken or vegetable stock
1 small green-fleshed melon,
  e.g. Galia
Juice of 1 small lemon
.4 Tbsp heavy cream

To serve:
Ice cubes

Peel the cucumber and cut in half lengthways. Using a teaspoon, scoop out the seeds. Chop the flesh and place in a saucepan. Pour over the stock, bring to a boil, cover and simmer gently for 10 minutes to soften. Remove from the heat and allow to cool.

Quarter the melon and scoop out the seeds, then slice off the skin. Cut the flesh into small pieces and place in a blender. Add the cooled cucumber, stock and lemon juice, and blend for a few seconds until smooth. Pour into a bowl, cover and chill for at least 2 hours.

Just before serving, stir in lemon juice to taste, and whisk in the heavy cream. Ladle into soup bowls and add a few ice cubes to serve.

Watermelon and crab salad

Oriental

An interesting mixture of flavors that packs a punch on the taste buds. It's colorful and healthy too. Leave the dressing ingredients to infuse together for a stronger flavor.

Serves 4

For the dressing:
2 Tbsp **freshly squeezed lime juice**
½-in (1-cm) piece **fresh ginger,** peeled and grated
2 Tbsp **fish sauce**
1 Tbsp **honey**
1 clove **garlic,** peeled and crushed
1 **small red chilli,** e.g. bird's eye, deseeded and finely chopped (optional)

For the salad:
¼ **small watermelon**
12oz (350g) **white crabmeat**
2 **shallots,** peeled and finely chopped
2 Tbsp **light soy sauce**
Juice and finely grated rind of 1 **lime**
1 head **bok choy,** trimmed
1 small bunch **coriander**
1 small bunch **Vietnamese basil**
1 small bunch **Vietnamese mint**

First make the dressing. Mix all the ingredients together; cover and set aside while you prepare the salad.

Slice off the peel from the watermelon, and cut the flesh into bite-sized pieces. Remove any seeds, and place the melon in a bowl. Carefully toss in the crabmeat and chopped shallots, and sprinkle over the soy sauce, lime juice and lime rind.

Break up the bok choy, rinse and shake dry. Rinse and shake dry the herbs and then roughly tear up the leaves. Toss into the bok choy.

To serve, pile the leaves and herbs onto four serving plates and top with the crab, watermelon, and juices. Serve with the dressing to drizzle over.

Green melon lassi, Watermelon cooler, Grape and ginger fizz

Thirst-quenching

Melons and grapes make a good base fruit for drinks; they are very versatile and mix well with many flavors. Here are three ideas to whet your appetite.

Each makes 1 drink

Green melon lassi:
¼ green-fleshed melon, e.g. Galia
Seeds from 1 green cardamom pod, crushed
⅔ cup (150ml) **whole-milk plain yogurt**

To serve:
Chilled water and ice cubes

Remove the seeds from the melon and slice off the skin. Place in a blender or food processor and add the cardamom and yogurt. Blend for a few seconds until smooth. Dilute with a little cold water if it is too thick. Pour into a glass over ice and serve immediately.

Watermelon cooler:
1 **thick slice watermelon**
Juice and finely grated rind of 1 lime
½-in (1-cm) **piece fresh ginger,** peeled and grated

To serve:
Chilled water and ice cubes

Remove the seeds from the melon and slice off the skin. Place in a blender or food processor and add the lime juice and rind, and ginger. Blend for a few seconds until smooth. Dilute with a little cold water if it is too thick. Pour into a glass over ice and serve immediately.

Grape fizz:
1¼ cups (150g) **seedless green grapes,** washed
Juice and finely grated rind of 1 lemon
⅔ cup (150ml) **dry ginger ale,** chilled

To serve:
Ice cubes

Place the grapes in a blender or food processor and add the lemon juice and rind. Blend for a few seconds until smooth. Dilute with ginger ale. Pour into a glass over ice and serve immediately.

Citrus fruit

Some of our most vibrant and sharp-tasting fruit fall into this chapter. Citrus fruit is all about fragrance: the heavenly, heady scent of the blossom on the trees, the pungency and uplifting aroma of the oil vapors as the skin is grated, and the wafting perfume as the juice is squeezed, all marry together to give us sensational fruitiness and value for money.

Oranges, limes and lemons are used all over the world in sweet and savory dishes alike, to give color and a zest that can invigorate even the simplest recipes. To enjoy these fruits at their best try the Fresh lime tart (see page 94) or the Lemony rice pudding (see page 102). For sheer intensity, a freshly made citrus fruit sorbet is probably one of the most flavorsome recipes you can make.

As well as recipes based on the more familiar of these fruits, I have included some using other members of the citrus family. Try the little orange kumquat, colored grapefruit, pungent tangerines, sweet and succulent minneolas and last but not least, the weird and wonderful ugli.

Fresh lime tart
Summertime

This is my all-time favorite citrus recipe, and is also very good made with lemons. The sharp-sweet combination makes a delicious dessert, which is excellent served with a tart fruit sauce such as raspberry.

Serves 6

For the pastry:
1½ cups (180g) **all-purpose flour**
1 pinch **salt**
½ cup (90g) **extra-fine sugar**
¾ stick (90g) **unsalted butter**
1 **egg yolk**
Few drops **vanilla extract**

For the filling:
4 **limes**, scrubbed
½ cup (115g) + 1 Tbsp **extra-fine sugar**
3 **eggs**, beaten
½ stick (60g) **unsalted butter**, melted

To serve:
Berry coulis (see page 155)

Preheat the oven to 400°F/200°C. For the pastry, sift the flour, salt and sugar into a bowl, and rub in the butter to form a mixture that resembles fresh breadcrumbs. Mix in the egg yolk and vanilla extract and bring the mixture together, then knead gently to form a firm dough. Wrap and chill for 30 minutes.

Meanwhile, make the filling. Using a vegetable peeler, pare off a few strips of zest from one of the limes, and cut into thin shreds. Simmer in a little water for about 5 minutes until tender. Drain well and pat dry with paper towel. Toss in 1 Tbsp sugar, then set aside in a warm place to dry.

Grate the rind from the remaining limes and extract the juice from all of them. Beat the rind, juice, sugar and eggs together. Cover and chill until required.

Roll out the pastry on a lightly floured surface to fit a 9-in/23-cm fluted loose-bottomed flan pan. The pastry is very short so you may find it easier to mold the pastry into the pan. Prick the base all over with a fork and bake in the oven for 12–15 minutes until lightly golden. Reduce the oven temperature to 350°F/180°C.

Whisk the melted butter into the lime filling and then pour into the pie case. Bake in the oven for a further 20 minutes until just set. Allow to cool in the pan, then remove from the pan and chill until required.

To serve, top the lime tart with the shredded lime zest. Serve with a Berry coulis (see page 155).

Fresh lime tart

Cuban-style candied citrus rind

Unusual

Citrus fruit grows in abundance in Cuba, and this is an old peasant dish which uses the fruit rind as a main ingredient. Serve two to three pieces per person, to accompany Gouda cheese.

Serves 8

1 unwaxed ugli fruit
1 unwaxed grapefruit
1 large unwaxed orange
Approx. 8 Tbsp salt
¼ cups (300g) granulated sugar
2½ cups (600ml) water

To serve:
Gouda cheese or cream cheese

Cut the ugli fruit into 6–8 equal segments, depending on size, and cut the grapefruit and orange into quarters. Slice the flesh away from the skin – use the flesh for fruit salads – and scrape away as much of the bitter white pith as possible from the inside of the skins. You may find a serrated knife helpful. Place the skin shells in a large bowl, sprinkle with 2 Tbsp salt and cover with water, then set aside for 24 hours, changing the salt water every few hours to remove the bitterness.

The next day, drain the shells and rinse thoroughly. Place in a large saucepan and cover with fresh cold water. Bring to a boil then discard the water, and repeat the process. This time, drain the shells, rinse well and set aside.

Place the sugar in a large saucepan and add the water. Cook over a low heat, stirring, until the sugar has dissolved. Bring to a boil, add the shells and bring back to a boil, then reduce the heat until simmering very gently. Cook, undisturbed, for about 2 hours until the shells are soft and transparent, and the liquid is syrupy, reduced by two-thirds, and thick.

Transfer the shells to a heatproof shallow dish and pour over the syrup. Allow to cool, then transfer to a serving dish, cover and chill for at least 2 hours before serving. Remove from the syrup to serve with wedges of Gouda or scoops of cream cheese.

■ *You can develop this recipe further to obtain candied dried fruit for baking. Once the rind has simmered in the syrup, allow it to cool as above, then remove using a slotted spoon and transfer to trays lined with baking parchment. Store in a warm, dry place, turning occasionally, for 3–4 days until dried. You can then cut up the rind according to your preference and store in an airtight jar until required.*

Orange poppy seed cake

Orange blossom

This is a great dessert, full of flavor and fragrance. It is a very close-textured cake, with the added richness of ground almonds. It is gluten-free so makes an indulgent treat for those on a restricted diet.

Serves 8

¾ cup (180ml) **light olive oil**
Scant 1 cup (180g) **extra-fine sugar**
2 **large eggs**
1 cup (150g) **ground almonds**
Finely grated rind of 1 **small orange**
Seeds from 4 **green cardamom pods**, crushed
Scant ¾ cup (90g) **polenta**
2 Tbsp **poppy seeds**
½ tsp **baking powder**

For the syrup:
¼ quantity **Sugar syrup** (see page 144)
Juice of 1 **small orange**
Few drops **orange flower water**

To serve:
4 **medium oranges**
Crème fraîche or **sour cream**

Preheat the oven to 350°F/180°C. Grease and line the base and sides of a 7-in (18-cm) springform cake pan with baking parchment.

Whisk together the olive oil, extra-fine sugar and eggs and then fold in the ground almonds, orange rind, cardamom, polenta, poppy seeds and baking powder. Spoon the mixture into the prepared pan and bake for 45–50 minutes until lightly golden and a skewer inserted into the center comes out clean.

While the cake is baking, prepare the syrup as directed on page 144. Remove the syrup from the heat and stir in the orange juice and a few drops of orange flower water to taste. Set aside.

Using a sharp knife, slice the top and bottom off the oranges, and slice off the peel taking away as much of the white pith as possible. Cut the oranges into thin slices. Remove any seeds and place on a plate. Sprinkle with a few drops of orange flower water, cover and chill until required.

When the cake comes out of the oven, skewer all over with a toothpick and pour the syrup over the warm cake. Allow to cool, then release from the pan. To serve, arrange the orange slices on top of the cake, and accompany with crème fraîche or sour cream.

Raisin pancakes with tangerine syrup

Comforting

Using tangerines gives these light and fluffy pancakes a really citrussy tang. You can use orange or lemon as an alternative.

Serves 4

1 cup (125g) **all-purpose flour**
2 tsp **baking powder**
½ tsp **baking soda**
1 tsp **extra-fine sugar**
2 **eggs**, separated
1 cup (250ml) **whole milk**
Finely grated rind of 1 **tangerine**
⅓ cup (60g) **golden raisins**
¼ stick (30g) **unsalted butter**

For the syrup:
½ **quantity Sugar syrup**
  (see page 144)
Finely grated rind and juice of
  2 **tangerines**
¼ stick (30g) **unsalted butter**

Sift the flour, baking powder, baking soda and sugar into a bowl and make a well in the center. Add the egg yolks, pour in the milk and gradually work into the flour using a whisk. Beat until thick and smooth, but take care not to over-mix.

In a grease-free bowl, whisk the egg whites until stiff and, using a large metal spoon, carefully fold into the batter together with the tangerine rind and raisins.

Heat a little butter in a large frying pan until bubbling, tilting the pan to coat the sides. Ladle ¼ cup (60ml) batter to form thick pancakes about 4in (10cm) in diameter. Cook over a low-to-moderate heat for about 2½ minutes, until bubbles appear on the surface. Turn over and cook for a further 2½ minutes until golden, puffed up and thick.

Turn the pancakes out onto a wire rack lined with a clean tea towel and baking parchment. Fold the paper and towel over the pancakes to keep them moist. Repeat this until you have used up all the batter and made eight pancakes in total, re-buttering the pan as necessary, and stacking the cooked pancakes between sheets of parchment until you are ready to serve.

For the syrup, make up as directed on page 144 but add the tangerine rind to the mixture before cooking. Add the butter and cool for 10 minutes. The butter will melt in the hot syrup. Stir in the tangerine juice and it will still be warm to serve poured over the pancakes.

Raisin pancakes with tangerine syrup

Trio of sorbets

Trio of sorbets

Refreshing

If you've had a heavy meal, sorbet is the perfect dessert solution. These sweet, zesty ices are just what's needed to lighten the palate and refresh your taste buds. They make a welcome cooling treat on a hot day.

Serves 4

1 quantity **Sugar syrup** (see page 144)

½ cup (125ml) **freshly squeezed blood orange juice** (approx. 2 medium blood oranges)

½ cup (125ml) **freshly squeezed lemon juice** (approx. 2½ medium lemons)

½ cup (125ml) **freshly squeezed minneola juice** (approx. 4 minneolas)

To serve:
Wafer-thin ginger crisps (see page 157)

Make up the sugar syrup as directed on page 144 and allow to cool completely.

Divide the syrup equally between the three fruit juices, and mix each well. Pour each of the citrus syrups into separate small freezer-proof containers and freeze until just beginning to freeze around the edges – this will take about 1 hour. Whisk well to break down the ice crystals evenly.

Return to the freezer and freeze for a further 1½–2 hours, whisking every 30 minutes, until firm. Cover and store in the freezer until required.

To serve, scoop or spoon the three sorbets into serving dishes and serve immediately. Ideal served with Wafer-thin ginger crisps (see page 157).

You can use this recipe to make other sorbets such as lime, pink grapefruit or traditional orange – simply substitute the juices.

Lemony rice pudding

Traditional

The simplest ingredients combine in this recipe to form a rich, creamy rice pudding. Lemon rind and "sweet" spices, vanilla and mace, give the subtle, comforting flavors we all know and love. Accompany with dried fruit compôte or with a hot cherry sauce.

Serves 6

2½ cups (600ml) **whole milk**
1 **small unwaxed lemon**
1¼ cups (90g) **short-grain pudding rice,** rinsed
1 **vanilla pod,** split down the center
3–4 **blades mace**
¼ cup (45g) **extra-fine sugar**
½ cup (60g) **golden raisins**
2 Tbsp **sweet sherry (optional)**
⅔ cup (150ml) **heavy cream**
¼ tsp **ground nutmeg (optional)**

Pour the milk in to a saucepan. Using a vegetable peeler, pare the rind of the lemon into the milk – you can use the juice in another recipe. Add the rice, vanilla pod and mace to the pan. Bring slowly to a boil, then simmer gently for 20 minutes, stirring occasionally, until the rice is soft and about two-thirds of the milk has been absorbed.

Stir in the sugar, raisins and sherry, if using. Cover loosely and set aside to cool. Discard the lemon rind, vanilla pod and mace.

Stir in the cream and transfer to a serving dish. Sprinkle with ground nutmeg if using and chill for 2 hours before serving with fruit.

Lemon-and-limeade

Thirst-quenching

This reminds me of lazy summer days, when the heat makes you feel drowsy. As I was growing up, my mom would make us iced fresh lemonade to cool us down and revive us. You can make this with just lemons if you prefer. If unwaxed fruit is unavailable, scrub the rind well with a vegetable brush.

Makes approx. 2pt (1.2L)

3 medium unwaxed lemons
3 unwaxed limes
1 cup (200g) **extra-fine sugar**
4½ cups (1L) **boiling water**

To serve:
Ice cubes
Lemon balm sprigs

Wash the lemons and limes thoroughly. Using a vegetable peeler, pare off the rind into a large heatproof bowl. Add the sugar and pour over the boiling water. Stir well and set aside to cool, stirring occasionally.

Extract the juice from the lemons and limes, and stir into the cooled liquid. Place a strainer over a serving pitcher and pour the liquid through. Cover and chill for at least 2 hours.

Serve well chilled, poured over ice, with a sprig of lemon balm for extra citrussy flavor.

■ *For a very quick version of this recipe, dissolve 1 Tbsp sugar in the juice of 1 lemon. Transfer to a glass and top up with chilled soda or mineral water to taste.*

Creamy lemon meringue pie

Family favorite

We would sometimes have lemon meringue pie as a special treat after a Sunday roast, and it was much anticipated by all of us. This version has more of a custard filling, giving the filling a velvety texture. Delicious!

Serves 6–8

10oz (300g) **ready-made basic pie dough (for 1 x 9in pie)**
4 Tbsp **cornstarch**
1¼ cups (275g) **extra-fine sugar**
Juice and finely grated rind of 2 **small lemons**
1¼ cups (300ml) **heavy cream**
2 **large eggs,** separated
1 **large egg white**
Shredded lemon rind, to decorate

To serve:
Light cream

Preheat the oven to 400°F/200°C. Roll out the pastry to fit a 1-in (2.5-cm) deep, 8-in (20-cm) round pie dish and lightly prick the base. Bake in the oven for 15 minutes until lightly golden. Set aside to cool.

Mix the cornstarch, scant ½ cup (125g) extra-fine sugar, lemon juice and rind together in a saucepan and add a little cream to form a paste. Stir in the remaining cream and cook over medium heat, stirring, until just boiling and thick. Cook for 1 minute longer then set aside to cool for 10 minutes. Stir in the egg yolks. Pour into the pie shell and cool completely.

In a large heatproof bowl, whisk the egg whites until stiff. Place the remaining sugar in a saucepan with ¼ cup (50ml) water and heat, stirring until the sugar has dissolved. Bring to a boil and cook until the temperature reads 240°F (121°C) on a sugar thermometer. Pour the hot syrup in a steady stream into the egg whites, and continue to whisk for a further 5 minutes. Spoon over the lemon filling to cover completely.

Preheat the broiler to medium. Cook the topping for 2–3 minutes until golden all over. Serve immediately, sprinkled with lemon rind, with light cream to accompany.

Creamy lemon meringue pie

Pink grapefruit gelatin desserts

Juicy

These delightfully pink gelatin desserts are light and healthy and are guaranteed to be a talking point. For a party, add 6 Tbsp vodka to the mixture to make a Sea Breeze cocktail dessert.

Serves 4

⅔ cup (150ml) **very hot water**
4 level tsp **Knox gelatin**
2 **pink grapefruit**
1¼ cups (300ml) **unsweetened pink grapefruit juice**
⅔ cup (150ml) **low-sugar cranberry juice**
4 Tbsp **thick sour cream**
Ground ginger, to taste

Pour the water into a heatproof basin and sprinkle over the gelatin. Stir until dissolved and set aside to cool for 30 minutes.

Meanwhile, using a sharp knife, slice the top and bottom off the grapefruit and slice off the peel, taking away as much of the white pith as possible. Holding the grapefruit over a bowl to catch the juices, slice in between each segment to remove the flesh, and place in the bowl. Cover and chill until required.

Once the gelatin mixture has cooled, stir in the grapefruit and cranberry juices along with the juices from the grapefruit segments.

Arrange a few segments in the bottom of four cocktail glasses or serving dishes and pour the gelatin mixture over the top. Place in the fridge to chill for at least 2 hours until set. To serve, spoon a dollop of sour cream on top of each and sprinkle with ground ginger.

Pink grapefruit gelatin desserts

Panforte

Fruit and nut

I remember sampling this Italian delicacy for the first time on a trip to Siena, where it is traditionally served as a Christmas cake. It was thickly dusted with confectioners sugar and wrapped in rice paper. I've since discovered that it's very easy to make and lovely to give as a present.

Cuts into 24 thin slices

Few sheets edible rice paper
½ cup (60g) **pine nuts,** toasted
½ cup (60g) **almonds,** blanched, toasted and chopped
1 cup (150g) **candied dried citrus rinds,** chopped **(see tip page 96)**
1 tsp **ground cinnamon**
½ cup (60g) **all-purpose flour**
⅓ cup (90g) **honey**
Generous ½ cup (90g) **light brown sugar**
3 Tbsp **icing sugar**

Preheat the oven to 300°F/150°C. Line the base and sides of an 8-in (20-cm) plain flan ring or tart pan with baking parchment and then add layers of rice paper, trimming as necessary, to cover the parchment.

In a heatproof bowl, mix the nuts, dried citrus rinds, cinnamon and flour together. Place the honey and sugar into a small saucepan and heat gently until the sugar melts. Bring to a boil, and then mix into the fruit and nut mixture to bind it together.

Press the mixture evenly into the prepared pan and bake for about 40 minutes until lightly golden. Allow to cool in the pan. Carefully remove, making sure that only the rice paper is stuck to the cake. Dust thickly with confectioners sugar. Wrap well to store. To serve, using a large sharp knife, cut into small wedges and eat as an after-dinner sweet treat.

Panforte

Carrot, red lentil and orange soup

Carrot, red lentil and orange soup

Hearty

Bright orange in color, this soup certainly packs a punch with its flavor as well as its vibrancy. It's thick and comforting, and is great served simply with crusty whole-wheat bread.

Serves 4

2 Tbsp **olive oil**
1 **onion,** peeled and chopped
1 **bay leaf**
2 sticks **celery,** trimmed and chopped
1lb (500g) **carrots,** peeled and
    chopped
½ cup (125g) **red lentils,** rinsed
14-oz (400-g) can **chopped tomatoes**
2½ cups (600ml) **vegetable stock**
Scant 1 cup (200ml) **freshly squeezed
    orange juice**
½ tsp **finely grated orange rind**
**Salt and freshly ground black
    pepper**
4 Tbsp **plain yogurt**
4 tsp **parsley,** chopped

Heat the oil in a large saucepan and gently fry the onion, bay leaf and celery for 5 minutes to soften slightly, but not brown. Add the carrots and cook, stirring for a further 2 minutes, until well coated in the onion and celery mixture.

Stir in the lentils, tomatoes and stock. Bring to a boil, cover and simmer for about 40 minutes, stirring occasionally, until thick and tender. Remove from the heat and leave to stand, covered, for 10 minutes. Discard the bay leaf.

Stir in the orange juice, rind and seasoning. Return to the heat, and reheat gently until piping hot but not boiling.

To serve, ladle into warmed soup bowls and swirl with yogurt. Sprinkle with chopped parsley and serve immediately.

Soft-bake marmalade cookies

Teatime treat

I love these chewy cookies, with their very zesty flavor. You'll need to use a sharp knife in order to cut the kumquats thinly so that they cook through during baking. Lovely drizzled with plain chocolate!

Makes 16

1½ cups (180g) **all-purpose flour**
1 pinch **salt**
½ cup (60g) **ground almonds**
¾ cup (125g) **light brown sugar**
¾ stick (90g) **unsalted butter**, cut into small pieces
1 **egg yolk**
6 Tbsp **fine-cut orange marmalade**
1–2 Tbsp **milk**
½ cup (90g) **kumquats,** thinly sliced

Preheat the oven to 350°F/180°C. Grease and line two large baking sheets with baking parchment.

Sift the flour and salt into a bowl and stir in the ground almonds and sugar. Rub in the butter until the mixture resembles fine breadcrumbs. Add the egg yolk and 3 Tbsp marmalade and bring the mixture together with enough milk to form a soft dough. Wrap and chill for 30 minutes.

Divide the mixture into 16 pieces, and gently roll each piece into a ball. Place on the baking sheets and press down to form rounds about 2in (5cm) in diameter. Gently press three slices of kumquat, overlapping, into the top of each cookie.

Soften the remaining marmalade with 1–2 tsp water and brush thickly over the top of each to glaze. Bake in the oven for 15–20 minutes until lightly golden and the kumquat slices are tender. Allow to cool on the baking sheets, then transfer to a serving plate.

Ceviche

Latin American

Popular all over South America, this healthy fish salad uses the acids in citrus juice to "cook" the fish. It is essential that the fish is very fresh and that it is left in the juices for sufficient time to allow this cooking process to happen.

Serves 4

8oz (250g) **skinless fresh white fish fillets, e.g. sole, cod or haddock**
Juice of 3 **limes** + 1 extra Tbsp **lime juice**
Juice of 1 **lemon**
1 **red onion,** peeled and thinly sliced
½ clove **garlic,** peeled and finely chopped
1 **green chilli,** deseeded and finely chopped
Salt and freshly ground black pepper
2 **small sweet potatoes**
2 **ripe avocadoes**
1 **Cos lettuce,** washed
1 **small bunch cilantro,** roughly chopped

Wash and pat dry the fish. Cut into ½-in (2-cm) pieces and place in a shallow, ceramic non-reactive dish – metal may affect the flavor of the fish.

Mix the juice of the three limes and the lemon juice with the onion, garlic, chilli and seasoning. Pour over the fish, making sure it is completely covered – add more juice if necessary. Cover and refrigerate overnight. The fish will look white and opaque when it is "cooked."

Peel the potatoes and cut into slices about ½in (1cm) thick. Place in a saucepan and cover with water. Bring to a boil and cook for 10–12 minutes until tender. Drain and allow to cool.

Halve the avocadoes and remove the stone. Peel away the skin and slice the flesh thinly. Sprinkle with the remaining lime juice, cover and chill until required.

When you are ready to serve, break up the lettuce and arrange on serving plates. Top with a few slices of sweet potato and avocado, and spoon over the marinated fish and juices. Serve immediately, sprinkled with cilantro.

Duck with sweet kumquat sauce

Duck with sweet kumquat sauce

Contemporary

An up-to-date twist on the classic French duck à l'orange. This vibrantly colored sauce is equally delicious served with roast chicken or pork. Try to use fresh, or a clear, light colored chicken stock to keep the color bright.

Serves 4

4 x 7-oz (200-g) **duck portions**
Salt and freshly ground black pepper
6 cloves **garlic,** peeled and halved
2 tsp **coriander seeds,** lightly crushed

For the sauce:
¼ stick (30g) **unsalted butter**
Generous ½ cup (125g) **kumquats,** thinly sliced
¼ cup (30g) **light brown sugar**
2 Tbsp (15g) **all-purpose flour**
Scant 1 cup (200ml) **freshly squeezed blood orange juice**
½ cup (100ml) **fresh chicken stock**

To serve:
Mashed potatoes
Green vegetables

Preheat the oven to 400°F/200°C. Wash and pat dry the duck portions and season all over. Make three small slits in the skin of each duck portion and push a piece of garlic in each. Arrange on a roasting rack over a roasting pan and sprinkle with coriander seeds. Bake in the oven for 35–40 minutes until richly golden and cooked through.

Meanwhile, make the sauce. Melt the butter in a saucepan until bubbling and add the kumquat slices. Cook, stirring, for 5 minutes until softened. Add the sugar and cook, stirring, for a further minute until syrupy, then blend in the flour. Remove from the heat and gradually blend in the orange juice and chicken stock. Return to the heat and cook gently, stirring, until simmering. Bring to a boil and cook gently for a further minute. Remove from the heat and remove any loose seeds that float to the top of the sauce. Set aside until you are ready to serve.

Drain the duck and place on warmed serving plates. Reheat the sauce if necessary and adjust the seasoning. Pour the sauce over the duck and accompany with creamy mashed potatoes and freshly cooked green vegetables.

■ *You can adapt this sauce to make a zingy accompaniment to a plain sponge cake: simply replace the stock with more orange juice and omit the seasoning.*

Ugli fruit, grapefruit and smoked fish salad

Ugli fruit, grapefruit and smoked fish salad

Bittersweet

A sophisticated salad or starter for grown-ups, this is an interesting combination of bitter leaves, tart fruit and sweet dressing. Ideal for a light lunch on a hot summer's day. Keep the fruit peel for the Cuban-style candied citrus rind recipe on page 96.

Serves 4

1 ugli fruit or pink grapefruit
1 pink or white grapefruit
1¼ cups (60g) **frisée lettuce or endive,** washed and roughly shredded
½ **radicchio lettuce,** trimmed, washed and roughly shredded
8oz (250g) **skinless smoked mackerel fillets,** flaked
3 Tbsp **unsweetened apple juice**
2 Tbsp **sunflower oil**
2 tsp **honey**
1 Tbsp **wholegrain mustard**
Salt and freshly ground black pepper

Using a sharp knife, slice the top and bottom off the ugli fruit and grapefruit, and slice off the peel, taking away as much of the white pith as possible. Holding the fruit over a bowl to catch the juices, slice between each segment to remove the flesh. Remove any seeds and place in a bowl. Cover and chill until required.

When you are ready to serve, mix the lettuces and pile onto four serving plates. Drain the citrus segments – the juice can be served separately if liked – and arrange on top of the leaves. Top with smoked mackerel. Mix the remaining ingredients together in a small jar and pour the dressing over the salads to serve.

Tropical and exotic fruit

We are so fortunate today to be able to enjoy fruits from all around the world that were once only eaten in their country of origin. A trip to any greengrocer or supermarket these days will set before us a veritable global feast of fruit.

In this chapter, I have selected fruits from Asia, the Caribbean, the Middle East and the warmer climates of the Mediterranean. All shapes, sizes, colors, fragrances and textures are set before you over the next few pages, guaranteed to whet your appetite, no matter what the occasion.

My personal favorites in this chapter are, first, the familiar banana – my parents can remember, as children, the excitement of seeing bananas for the first time in Britain after World War ii; it hardly seems possible to imagine life without them now. I'm sure you'll love the Banana pudding cake (see page 125). I also love the sweet pungency of passion fruit – it makes a delicious ice cream. Finally, there is the pomegranate – when the flesh is bright red, juicy and sweet, no other fruit comes close. The juice makes a very refreshing drink. Plenty of other exotic fruits are included as well, and I hope you enjoy trying them out in your cooking.

Baked papaya with ginger and lime

Baked papaya with ginger and lime

Pink

A perfectly ripe papaya has delicate flowery-flavored flesh which needs very little additional flavoring. I've found that ginger and lime are two of the best accompaniments to this luscious fruit. They are also good complements for mangoes and bananas.

Serves 4

2 large ripe papayas
2 small pieces **preserved ginger plus 1 Tbsp preserving syrup from the jar**
½ stick (45g) **unsalted butter,** softened
2 Tbsp **caster sugar**
1 **lime**

To serve:
Low-fat plain yogurt

Preheat the oven to 350°F/180°C. Halve the papayas lengthways and scoop out the central black seeds using a teaspoon. Place side by side in a baking dish or small roasting pan.

Finely chop the ginger and mix into the butter along with the syrup from the ginger jar and sugar. Divide between the cavities of the papaya halves.

Grate the rind from the lime and sprinkle a little over each papaya half. Extract the juice and drizzle over. Bake in the oven, basting occasionally with the juices, for 25 minutes until tender. Serve the papaya halves hot, with low-fat plain yogurt.

Tropical fruit bombe

Sensational

This dessert will make a stunning finale to a special meal or dinner party. If you don't have a specialist bombe mold, then you can use a small mixing bowl. All the layers can be served separately in their own right if preferred – see the tip below.

Serves 10

For the ice creams:
1 quantity **Sugar syrup** (see page 144)
6 **large ripe passion fruit**
2 **large ripe bananas**
1 Tbsp **freshly squeezed lemon juice**
1¼ cups (300ml) **heavy cream**

For the sorbets:
1 quantity **Sugar syrup** (see page 144)
1 **large ripe mango**
2 Tbsp **freshly squeezed lime juice**
4 **ripe kiwi fruit**
2 Tbsp **freshly squeezed lemon juice**

To decorate
Whipped cream and iced star fruit slices (see tip below)

Chill a 6-cup (1.4-L) bombe mold or small bowl in the freezer overnight. For the ice creams, make up the sugar syrup as directed on page 144 and allow to cool completely.

Cut the passion fruit in half and scoop out the seeds and flesh. Strain the juice into a bowl, rubbing the seeds through a nylon sieve to remove as much flesh as possible – you should have about ¼ cup (75ml) juice. Stir in about 2 tsp seeds if liked, and discard the remaining seeds. Peel and mash the bananas in a bowl and mix with the lemon juice – you should have about 1 cup (200g) mashed fruit.

Divide the syrup equally between the two fruit purées, and mix each well. Pour into separate, small, freezer-proof containers and freeze until just beginning to ice around the edges – about 1–1½ hours. Whisk well to break down the ice crystals evenly.

Whip the cream until just peaking and fold into the frozen fruit purées. Return to the freezer and freeze for a further 1½–2 hours, whisking every

30 minutes, until firm. Cover and store in the freezer until required.

For the sorbets, make up the sugar syrup as directed on page 144 and allow to cool completely.

Peel the skin from the mango. Slice down either side of the smooth flat central stone and place the flesh in a blender or food processor together with the lime juice – you should have about 1¼ cups (300g) flesh. Blend for a few seconds until smooth. Transfer to a bowl. Peel the kiwi fruit and chop roughly – you should have about 1¼ cups (300g) flesh. Place in a blender or food processor with the lemon juice and blend for a few seconds until smooth. Transfer to another bowl.

Divide the syrup equally between the two fruit purées, and mix each well. Pour into separate, small, freezer-proof containers and freeze until just beginning to freeze around the edges – about 1–1½ hours. Whisk well to break down the ice crystals evenly. Return to the freezer and freeze for a further 1½–2 hours, whisking every 30 minutes, until firm. Cover and store in the freezer until required.

To assemble the bombe, remove the ice creams and sorbets from the freezer and stand at room temperature for about 20 minutes to soften slightly. Spoon enough of the banana ice cream into the bottom of the mold to fill a quarter of the space, and smooth the top to form a neat layer. Top with passion fruit ice cream to come halfway up the mold, then kiwi sorbet to fill three-quarters and, finally, enough mango sorbet to fill the mold to the top. Place a layer of wax paper on top and cover with the lid or foil. Freeze for at least 12 hours. Return the remaining ice cream and sorbet to the freezer and store for up to 3 months.

To serve, dip the mold or bowl in hot water for a few seconds to loosen and invert onto a serving platter. Decorate the bombe with whipped cream and star fruit slices. To slice, dip the blade of a sharp knife in very hot water, dry and then slice through the layers like a cake.

■ *Cut 2 ripe star fruits into ½-in (1-cm) thick slices and place on trays lined with baking parchment. Open-freeze until required, and then serve as an iced fruit decoration for sorbets and ice creams.*

It is quite difficult, and time-consuming, to make small quantities of ice cream and sorbets, so this recipe makes more than sufficient for the mold – you will have extra left over to serve as you please.

Banana pudding cake

Banana pudding cake

Warming

You can serve this comforting creation as a pudding with Custard sauce (see page 145) or Toffee sauce (see page 145), or – if you can! – let it cool a little and serve a warm slice with tea.

Serves 8

2 sticks (225g) **unsalted butter**
1¾ cups (275g) **dark brown sugar**
3 **large ripe bananas**
4 **eggs**, beaten
1 tsp **vanilla extract**
1 cup (100g) **self-rising flour**
½ tsp **ground allspice**
1 pinch **salt**
Generous ½ cup (90g) **ground almonds**

Preheat the oven to 350°F/180°C. Melt 1 stick (100g) butter in a saucepan and, when bubbling, add 1 cup (150g) of the sugar. Simmer gently for about 3 minutes, stirring occasionally, until syrupy. Pour into the base of a 9-in (23-cm) round cake pan.

Peel the bananas, cut two in half, and then slice through lengthways. Fan the banana slices in a round over the base of the pan. Set aside. Mash the remaining banana.

In a mixing bowl, cream together the remaining butter and sugar together until pale, and fluffy in texture. Gradually whisk in the eggs with the vanilla and half the flour. Sift in the remaining flour, ground allspice and salt and add the ground almonds. Fold in together with the mashed banana until well mixed and then pile on top of the fanned-out bananas.

Smooth over the top and bake in the oven for 40–45 minutes until lightly golden and firm to the touch. Cool in the pan for 10 minutes to serve hot, or allow to cool for longer before turning out to serve warm.

Honey and rosemary roast figs

Fragrant

When figs are at their best, I like to eat them as part of a salad with cheeses and wafer-thin ham. If you bake them with a little honey and some herbs, you'll bring out even more of their natural sweetness.

Serves 4

8 large ripe figs
2 Tbsp honey
6 Tbsp unsweetened grape or apple
 juice
6oz (180g) feta cheese
Few sprigs fresh rosemary plus extra
 to garnish

To serve:
Thinly sliced smoked ham
Fresh bread

Preheat the oven to 375°F/190°C. Halve the figs and place in a shallow ovenproof dish. Blend the honey and juice together and pour over the figs.

Crumble the cheese and sprinkle over the figs. Scatter with rosemary sprigs. Bake in the oven for about 20 minutes, basting occasionally, until tender. Allow to cool.

To serve, drain the figs, reserving the juice, and transfer to serving plates. Spoon over the cooking juices, garnish, and serve with smoked ham and bread to mop up the juices.

Honey and rosemary roast figs

Fragrant fruit skewers

Contemporary

These look fantastic and are a great way to encourage the kids to eat fruit. The intriguing shapes and colors should get everyone interested in trying them. You can, of course, vary the fruits you put on the skewers.

Serves 4

2 ripe persimmons (sharon fruit)
2 ripe star fruit (carambola)
1 small ripe papaya
2 ripe guavas
Juice of 1 lemon
1 small ripe mango
4 Tbsp freshly squeezed
   orange juice
⅔ cup (150ml) whole-milk
   plain yogurt
6 Tbsp reduced-fat coconut milk
2 Tbsp extra-fine sugar

Peel the persimmons, then quarter the flesh. Wash the star fruit and cut into ½-in (1-cm) thick slices. Peel the papaya, halve it and scoop out the seeds. Cut the flesh into pieces about ¾in (2cm) thick. Peel the guavas, quarter them and remove the seeds, if preferred.

Thread the pieces of fruit alternately on to eight skewers and place in a shallow dish. Sprinkle with lemon juice, cover and chill for 30 minutes.

Meanwhile, peel the skin from the mangoes. Slice down either side of the smooth flat central stone and place in a blender or food processor with the orange juice. Blend for a few seconds until smooth and pulpy. Mix the yogurt, coconut milk and sugar together and transfer to a serving bowl. Gently swirl the mango purée into the yogurt mixture to give a rippled effect. Cover and chill until required.

To serve, remove the skewers from the fridge about 20 minutes before serving – the flavors will be stronger if you do this – and serve with the bowl of mango and coconut yogurt for dipping.

Fragrant fruit skewers

Date crumble bars
Sticky-sweet

Dates have a natural intense sweetness and sticky texture, which makes them the perfect filling for pastries or tarts. Try serving these bars cold as a teatime treat or warm with custard.

Makes 12

1½ cups (350g) **fresh dates, stoned and chopped**
⅔ cup (150ml) **freshly squeezed orange juice**
1½ sticks (180g) **butter, softened**
¾ cup (100g) **light brown sugar**
Generous 1 cup (125g) **rolled oats**
1½ cups (180g) **self-rising flour**

Preheat the oven to 350°F/180°C. Grease and line a 7 x 11-in (18 x 28-cm) cake pan. Put the dates in a saucepan with the orange juice. Bring to a boil, cover and simmer gently for 5 minutes to soften. Remove from the heat, mash until smooth and set aside to cool.

In a mixing bowl, beat together the butter and sugar, and then stir in the oats and flour to form a crumbly mixture. Press half into the base of the prepared pan to form a smooth base. Prick all over with a fork and bake for 10–12 minutes until lightly golden.

Spread the date paste over the cooked base and sprinkle with the remaining crumble topping. Bake for 30 minutes until lightly golden. Cut into 12 bars and allow to cool in the pan.

Jeweled lychees

Exotic

A simple variation of a fruit salad, full of gentle flavors. It takes a bit of time to prepare but will be greatly admired served as a light dessert at an Oriental-themed dinner party.

Serves 4

1 tsp **good-quality Japanese green tea leaves**
⅔ cup (150ml) **boiling water**
2 **star anise**
1 **stalk lemongrass,** trimmed and the bulb chopped
1 Tbsp **extra-fine sugar**
2 Tbsp **dry sherry (optional)**
4 cups (500g) **lychees**
1 **kiwi fruit,** peeled
1 thick slice **papaya,** skinned and deseeded
1 thick slice **pineapple,** skin and core removed

Place the tea leaves in a small heatproof bowl and pour over the boiling water. Brew for 3 minutes then strain away the leaves. Add the star anise and lemongrass, and stir in the sugar until dissolved. Set aside to cool, then strain, add the sherry, if using, then cover and chill until required.

Peel the lychees and carefully prize out the stones without cutting them in half. Cut the kiwi fruit, papaya and pineapple into small pieces and push one piece of fruit inside each lychee. Cover and chill until required. Mix any remaining fruit together, cover and chill, and keep for serving with the lychees.

To serve, arrange a selection of stuffed lychees on each serving plate, along with the reserved chopped fruits, and spoon over the prepared syrup.

Cuban fruit salad

Colorful

The endless variety of fruits in Cuba make varied appearances in salad form. This is one of the more unusual salads.

Serves 6

2 ripe star fruit (carambola)
½ medium ripe pineapple
2 large oranges
1 pink grapefruit
2 large ripe tomatoes
Juice of 2 limes
1 tsp **lime rind,** finely grated
1 Tbsp **honey**
2 Tbsp **light rum (optional)**
1 Tbsp **chopped mint**
⅔ cup (150ml) **canned coconut milk**
4 Tbsp **Sugar syrup (see page 144)**

Wash and thinly slice the star fruit and place in a bowl. Remove the skin from the pineapple and chop the flesh, and add to the bowl.

Using a sharp knife, slice off the top and bottom from the oranges. Slice off the skin, taking away as much of the white pith as possible. Holding the peeled fruit over the bowl, slice out the segments of orange flesh and let them fall into the bowl along with the juices. Repeat this with the grapefruit.

Quarter the tomatoes and remove the seeds. Using a sharp knife, slice the flesh from the skin, then roughly chop and add to the fruit.

Mix the lime juice and rind with the honey and rum, if using. Pour over the fruit, cover and chill for 1 hour before serving sprinkled with freshly chopped mint. Mix the coconut milk and sugar syrup together and chill until required. Serve the fruit with the chilled, sweetened coconut milk to pour over.

Cuban fruit salad

Guava pastries

Melt-in-the-mouth

These crumbly, soft pastries are filled with thick Guava cheese (see page 146) but you can use your favorite jam instead. Serve with a cup of dark, black coffee – lovely!

Makes 16

2 cups (215g) **all-purpose flour plus extra for dusting**
1 tsp **salt**
1 Tbsp **extra-fine sugar**
1½ sticks (180g) **unsalted butter, softened**
¾ cup (180g) **cream cheese**
1 cup (250g) **Guava cheese (see page 146)**
1 **egg white,** lightly beaten
2 Tbsp **granulated sugar**
Ground cinnamon, for dusting

Preheat the oven to 400°F/200°C. Sift the flour, salt and extra-fine sugar into a bowl, and either by hand or using an electric mixer, beat in the butter and cream cheese to form a soft dough. Cover and chill for 30 minutes.

Lightly dust a work surface with flour. Divide the dough into four equal pieces to make it easier to work with. Taking one piece of dough at a time, roll out to form an 8-in (20-cm) square. Cut into four smaller squares.

Place a teaspoon of the guava cheese in the center of each square, and brush the edges lightly with water. Gently fold the pastry over, and secure the edges by pressing with a fork. Lightly slash the top with a sharp knife.

Place the pastries on baking sheets, about 2in (5cm) apart, cover loosely and chill for 30 minutes.

Brush lightly with the beaten egg white and sprinkle lightly with the sugar and cinnamon. Bake for about 25 minutes until golden and crisp. Serve while still warm.

Tropical fruit platter

Rainbow-colored

A simple pinch of spice, some extra sweetness and the juice of citrus can transform any firm-fleshed fruit into something extra special. This is an excellent dessert for sharing, and to put the fun back into eating healthily.

Serves 4 to 6

1 baby (queen) pineapple
1 small ripe papaya
1 small ripe mango
2 kiwi fruit
2 ripe guavas
4 apple (finger) bananas
4 Tbsp **dark rum or orange juice**
1 tsp **ground allspice**
2 Tbsp **freshly squeezed lime juice**
4 Tbsp **dark brown sugar**
1 quantity Toffee sauce (see page 145) hot, to serve

Quarter the pineapple, remove the skin and trim away most of the leaves. Peel the papaya, scoop out the seeds and cut into thick wedges. Peel the skin from the mangoes. Slice down either side of the smooth flat central stone and cut the flesh into thick wedges. Peel the kiwi fruit and cut in half. Peel and halve the guavas – scoop out the seeds if preferred. Place all the fruit in a large dish. Sprinkle over the rum or orange juice, allspice and lime juice. Cover and stand at room temperature for 30 minutes, basting occasionally.

Preheat the broiler to hot. Drain the fruit, reserving the juices, and arrange on the broiler pan. Sprinkle with the brown sugar and cook for 4–5 minutes until hot, bubbling and just beginning to brown. Transfer to a warm serving platter and spoon over the reserved juices. Serve with hot toffee sauce.

Pineapple and banana fritters
Comforting

The natural juices exude from these fruit slices when they are encased in light, crispy batter and deep-fried. Serve sprinkled with extra-fine sugar flavored with ground cinnamon and a dollop of whipped cream or ice cream.

Serves 4

2 **baby (queen) pineapples**
2 **large ripe bananas**
6 Tbsp **self-rising flour**
1 **pinch salt**
⅔ cup (150ml) **canned coconut milk**
Vegetable oil, for deep-frying
4 Tbsp **extra-fine sugar**
½ tsp **ground cinnamon**

To serve:
Whipped cream or ice cream

Peel the pineapple and cut into ¾-in (2-cm) thick round slices. Peel the bananas, cut in half and then slice through lengthways. Set aside.

Sift the flour and salt in a small bowl and gradually mix in the coconut milk to form a smooth batter.

Heat the oil for deep-frying to 375°F (190°C). Dip the slices of fruit in the batter and fry four to five slices at a time for 3–4 minutes until crisp and golden. Drain on paper towel.

To serve, mix the sugar and cinnamon together and sprinkle over the fruit fritters. Serve immediately, with whipped cream or ice cream.

Passion fruit and coconut milk puddings

Rich

I used to love milk puddings as a child, and this pre-school favorite gave me the idea for the following recipe. The intensity of passion fruit combined with the crunchy seeds makes for an ideal accompaniment to creamy coconut.

Serves 4

2½ cups (600ml) **canned coconut milk**
¼ cup (75g) **cornstarch**
¼ tsp **ground cinnamon**
¼ tsp **ground allspice**
Scant ½ cup (75g) **extra-fine sugar**
4 **ripe passion fruit**

Blend a little of the milk with the cornstarch to form a smooth paste. Pour the remaining milk into a saucepan and stir in the paste and add the cinnamon, allspice and sugar. Stirring all the time, heat the mixture to boiling point and then cook for 2 minutes, taking care not to burn the mixture on the bottom of the saucepan – the mixture will be very thick.

Spoon the mixture into four ⅔-cup (150-ml) lightly oiled custard cups, smooth off the tops and set aside to cool. Then chill for at least 2 hours.

To serve, loosen the puddings from the cups by prizing the pudding away from the sides of the cup, and then upturning onto serving plates and shaking to release. Halve the passion fruit and scoop out the seeds. Spoon the seeds over the pudding and serve.

Tropical drinks

Tropical drinks

Healthy

Making drinks and smoothies from ripe fruit is an excellent way to help you meet your recommended daily intake. These virtuous concoctions will certainly make you feel better inside without trying too hard!

Each makes 1 drink

Green energy juice:
1 ripe kiwi fruit
6 lychees
½-in (1-cm) piece **fresh gingerroot,**
  peeled and roughly chopped
⅔ cup (150ml) **cold green tea, chilled**

Peel and roughly chop the kiwi fruit. Place in a blender or food processor. Peel and halve the lychees; remove the seeds and add to the blender together with the ginger. Pour over the cold tea and blend for a few seconds until smooth. Dilute with a little cold water if too thick, and serve immediately.

Pomegranate and persimmon
  (sharon fruit) yogurt drink:
1 large ripe pomegranate
2 ripe persimmons (sharon fruit)
½ cup (100ml) **plain yogurt**
½ tsp **rosewater**

To serve:
Few ice cubes

Halve the pomegranate and gently juice using a citrus reamer (see page 13). Pour the juice into a blender or food processor. Halve the persimmons and scoop the flesh into the blender. Add the yogurt and rosewater. Blend for a few seconds until smooth. Pour over ice cubes and serve immediately.

Banana and papaya smoothie:
1 ripe banana
½ small ripe papaya
⅔ cup (150ml) **milk or soy milk,**
  chilled
1–2 tsp **honey,** to taste
1 pinch **cinnamon or nutmeg**

Peel and roughly chop the banana. Place in a blender or food processor. Scoop out the seeds from the papaya, and remove the skin. Chop roughly and add to the blender along with the other ingredients. Blend for a few seconds until smooth and thick. Serve immediately.

Mango and lamb brochettes

Indian take-out

This is my version of a favorite Indian dish, Tikka. It is low-fat, and the yogurt helps tenderize the lamb as it marinades. You can use chicken fillet instead of lamb if you prefer.

Serves 4

1lb (500g) **lean boneless lamb**
1 clove **garlic,** crushed
½-in (1-cm) piece **fresh gingerroot,** peeled and grated
1 **green chilli,** deseeded and finely chopped
2 tsp **mild curry powder**
1 Tbsp **tomato paste**
3 Tbsp **freshly squeezed lemon juice**
6 Tbsp **whole-milk plain yogurt**
Salt and freshly ground black pepper
1 **large ripe mango**

For the salsa:
1 **large ripe mango**
1 **small red onion,** peeled and finely chopped
¼ **cucumber,** finely chopped
3 Tbsp **mint,** chopped

Wash and pat dry the lamb. Trim away any excess fat and then cut into 1-in (2.5-cm) thick pieces and place in a bowl.

Mix together the garlic, ginger, chilli, curry powder, tomato paste, 1 Tbsp lemon juice and the yogurt. Season well. Mix into the lamb and coat well. Cover and chill for at least 2 hours.

Meanwhile, peel the skin from the mangoes. Slice down either side of the smooth flat central stone and cut the flesh from the mango into 1-in (2.5-cm) pieces. Cover and chill until required.

To make the salsa, finely chop the flesh from the second mango and mix together the onion, cucumber and mint. Cover and chill until required.

Thread the lamb with pieces of mango alternately onto eight skewers and arrange on a broiler rack. Brush with any yogurt mixture that remains in the bowl.

Preheat the broiler to moderate, and cook the skewers for about 15 minutes, turning occasionally, until tender and slightly pink, or cook longer to your liking. Serve the skewers with the prepared salsa.

■ *If you are using wooden skewers, soak them for at least 30 minutes beforehand to avoid burning them.*

Mango and lamb brochettes

Date and eggplant pilaf

Date and eggplant pilaf

Middle-Eastern

You can serve this eye-catching dish as a vegetarian meal on its own or as a side dish to a lamb casserole.

Serves 4 to 6

1 lb (500g) **eggplants**
Approx. 3 Tbsp **salt**
½ stick (60g) **unsalted butter**
4 Tbsp **olive oil**
1 tsp **cumin seeds,** lightly crushed
1 tsp **coriander seeds,** lightly crushed
1 **small cinnamon stick,** broken
1 generous pinch **saffron**
1 **large onion,** peeled and chopped
1 clove **garlic,** peeled and finely
   chopped
2½ cups (250g) **basmati rice,** rinsed
3¾ cups (800ml) **boiling water**
Scant 1 cup (200g) **fresh dates,**
   stoned and chopped
6 Tbsp **chopped parsley**
Freshly ground black pepper
Seeds from 1 **ripe pomegranate**

Trim the eggplant and cut into ½ in (1cm) pieces. Layer in a colander or large strainer, sprinkling with salt, and set aside over a bowl for 30 minutes. This helps to extract the water, which softens the flesh as it cooks. Rinse well and pat dry with paper towel.

Meanwhile, melt the butter with the oil in a large saucepan until bubbling and then gently fry the spices for 2 minutes. Add the onion and garlic and cook gently for 5 minutes. Add the eggplant and stir-fry for 5 minutes. Stir in the rice and coat well in the onion mixture.

Pour in the water, bring to a boil, half-cover and simmer for 8–10 minutes until the rice is just tender. Turn off the heat and stir in the dates. Cover and leave to stand for 30 minutes until the liquid has been absorbed.

To serve, stir in the parsley and season with black pepper. Pile the pilaf into a warmed serving dish and sprinkle generously with the pomegranate seeds.

Preserves, sauces and accompaniments

Sugar syrup

Makes approx. 2½ cups (600ml)

Scant 1½ cups (350g) **extra-fine sugar**
2½ cups (600ml) **cold water**

Place the sugar in a saucepan and pour over the water. Heat, stirring, until the sugar dissolves. Increase the heat and bring to a boil. Simmer, without stirring, for 10 minutes. Remove from the heat and allow to cool.

■ *For citrus-flavored syrups, add citrus rind to the mixture before cooking; for sweet-spice syrups, add a cinnamon stick, coriander seeds, star anise, ginger, etc. to the mixture before cooking; and for a vanilla syrup, cook the mixture first before adding 2 split vanilla pods to the mixture, and leave until cool. A few drops of rosewater and orange flower water can also be added to cold syrup for fragrance.*

Custard sauce

Makes approx. 2½ cups (600ml)

4 level Tbsp **cornstarch**
3 Tbsp **extra-fine sugar**
2½ cups (600ml) **whole milk**
2 **egg yolks**
Few drops **vanilla extract**
Few drops **yellow food coloring (optional)**

In a saucepan, blend the cornstarch with a little of the milk to make a smooth paste. Stir in the sugar and remaining milk. Heat, stirring, over the heat until boiling and thick – you may find it easier to use a whisk to help keep the mixture smooth. Cook for 2 minutes.

Remove from the heat and cool for 10 minutes. Stir in the egg yolks and return to the heat. Cook through for 3 minutes, stirring, but without boiling. Add vanilla extract to taste, and color with food coloring if liked. To use cold, pour into a heatproof bowl and cover the surface with wax paper to prevent a skin forming. Allow to cool before covering and chilling until required.

For a thicker custard, use 1 Tbsp more cornstarch.

Toffee sauce

Makes approx. 2 cups (450ml)

⅔ cup (150g) **corn syrup**
½ stick (60g) **unsalted butter**
1 cup (150g) **dark brown sugar**
⅔ cup (150ml) **heavy cream**
Few drops **vanilla extract**

Put the syrup, butter and sugar in a saucepan and heat gently, stirring, until the sugar dissolves. Bring to simmering point and cook for 5 minutes. Remove from the heat and gradually stir in the cream and vanilla extract to taste. Serve hot or cold.

For a lighter, caramel-flavored sauce, use light brown sugar instead.

Quince (or Guava) cheese

Makes approx. 6¼ cups (1.5kg) quince; approx. 4½ cups (1kg) guava

2½lb (1.25kg) **ripe quinces**
2 cups (450ml) **water**
5¼ cups (900g) **granulated sugar**
3 tsp **finely grated lemon rind**
6 Tbsp **freshly squeezed lemon juice**

Peel and core the quinces. Cut into small pieces and place in a saucepan. Pour over the water. Bring to a boil, cover and simmer for 8–10 minutes until soft.

Remove the lid and cook for a further 20 minutes until thick, stirring occasionally to prevent sticking. Push through a nylon sieve or strainer to form a purée. Return to the saucepan and add the sugar, lemon rind and juice. Stir over low heat until the sugar has dissolved. Bring to a boil and cook steadily for about 30–40 minutes until rich, pinkish orange in color and very thick – stir occasionally to keep the mixture from sticking to the bottom of the saucepan.

Spoon into a large bowl or individual dishes and cover tightly. To store, spoon into small, hot jars and seal as described on page 15. To serve, turn out of the bowl, dish or jar and slice, or serve straight from the dish with a spoon.

■ *For guava cheese, peel 2½lb (1.25kg) ripe guavas and roughly chop the flesh and pulp. Weigh and place in a saucepan. Add 8fl oz (250ml) water per 1lb (500g) prepared fruit. Follow the steps above, using 1¼ cups (300g) white sugar and 1 Tbsp lemon juice per 1¼ cups (300ml) purée (omit the lemon rind). The guava cheese will be a deep golden yellow color.*

Apricot conserve

Makes approx. 3 cups (750g)

1lb (500g) **ripe apricots**
2¼ cups (500g) **granulated sugar**
2½ Tbsp **lemon juice**

Halve the apricots and remove the stones. Crack the stones using a rolling pin and tie them in a muslin bag. Place the apricots and stones in a bowl and mix in the sugar and lemon juice. Allow to stand for 15 minutes only, stirring occasionally, to allow the flavors to develop, but not allowing the fruit to discolor.

Transfer to a saucepan and heat gently until the sugar has dissolved, stirring all the time. Remove the stone bag, increase the heat and cook steadily until the setting point is reached – see page 15. Allow to cool slightly, stir to distribute the fruit, then spoon into hot jars and seal as described on page 15.

■ *Follow the quantities and method above using plums, peaches or nectarines.*

Summer berry jam

Makes approx. 4½ cups (1kg)

1 cup (250g) **strawberries,** hulled and roughly chopped
3¼ cups (680g) **granulated sugar**
4 Tbsp **freshly squeezed lemon juice**
1 cup (250g) **alpine strawberries,** hulled
1 cup (250g) **blueberries**

Place the ordinary strawberries on their own in a saucepan and heat gently until hot, then stir in the sugar and lemon juice. Stir over low heat until the sugar has dissolved, then stir in the alpine strawberries and blueberries. Increase the heat and boil rapidly until the setting point is reached – see page 15. Spoon into hot jars and seal as described on page 15.

■ *If alpine strawberries are unavailable, substitute with 1 cup (250g) raspberries or just use 2 cups (500g) strawberries.*

Bramble (blackberry) jelly

Makes approx. 3 cups (750g)

4 cups (1kg) **blackberries,** washed and hulled
⅔ cup (150ml) **water**
Approx. 2¼ cups (500g) **granulated sugar**
Approx. 2 Tbsp **freshly squeezed lemon juice**

Place the blackberries in a large saucepan and add the water. Bring to a boil and simmer for 10 minutes until very soft, pressing the fruit occasionally.

Strain the fruit and its juices through a jelly bag or some clean muslin suspended over a clean bowl – this will take about 6 hours to allow the fruit left behind to become dry. Don't be tempted to squeeze the mixture.

Measure the juice and pour back into the saucepan. Add 2¼ cups (500g) sugar and 2 Tbsp lemon juice per 2½ cups (600ml) blackberry juice. Heat, stirring, over low heat until the sugar has dissolved. Increase the heat and boil rapidly for about 15 minutes until the setting point is reached – see page 15. Skim off any surface foam using a flat spoon. Pour into hot jars and seal as described on page 15.

Grapefruit marmalade

Makes approx. 9 cups (2kg)

1lb (500g) **unwaxed ruby, pink or white grapefruit (approx.** 2 **medium fruit)**
6¼ cups (1.5L) **cold water**
7¼ cups (1.25kg) **granulated sugar**
5 Tbsp **lemon juice**

Halve the fruit and extract the juice, reserving the seeds and membranes that get caught in the juicer. Using a serrated grapefruit knife or spoon, scrape away and reserve the white pith from inside the grapefruit shells.

Tie the reserved seeds, membrane and pith in a piece of muslin and place in a bowl. Finely shred the grapefruit shells and place in the bowl. Pour over the cold water. Cover and leave to soak overnight in a cool place. Cover and chill the juice until required.

The next day, transfer the contents of the bowl to a large saucepan, bring to a boil and simmer for about 20 minutes until soft. Discard the muslin bag, and stir in the sugar, lemon juice, and reserved grapefruit juice. Stir over low heat until the sugar dissolves, then increase the heat and boil rapidly until the setting point is reached – see page 15. Cool for 15 minutes then stir to distribute the peel. Spoon into hot jars and seal as described on page 15.

■ *To use ugli fruit, follow the method above but increase lemon juice quantity to 6 Tbsp.*

Mango chutney

Makes approx. 3 cups (750g)

1½lb (750g) **just-ripe prepared mango flesh** (approx. 2 **large whole mangoes**)
⅔ cup (150ml) **white vinegar**
2 cloves **garlic,** peeled
1-in (2.5-cm) piece **fresh gingerroot,** peeled
Seeds from 4 **green cardamom pods,** crushed
6 **black peppercorns**
1 **bay leaf**
2 **dried hot red chillies**
1¼ cups (280g) **granulated sugar**
2 Tbsp **lemon juice**
½ tsp **toasted mustard seeds**
½ tsp **toasted cumin seeds**
1 tsp **black onion seeds**
Salt (optional)

Place the prepared and weighed mango flesh in a saucepan and pour over the vinegar. Tie the garlic and ginger along with the spices, bay leaf and chillies in a piece of muslin and add to the saucepan. Bring to a boil, cover and simmer for about 15 minutes, stirring occasionally and lightly mashing, until just tender.

Add the sugar and lemon juice, and stir until dissolved. Increase the heat and boil steadily for 20–25 minutes until the mixture is the consistency of a soft jam. Leave to stand for 10 minutes.

Remove the spice bag, stir in the seeds and season with salt if you wish. Spoon into hot jars and seal as described on page 15.

■ *To toast the mustard and cumin seeds, fry in a small frying pan for about 1 minute.*

Lemon curd

Makes approx. 2 cups (500g)

3 unwaxed medium lemons
1¼ cups (250g) **extra-fine sugar**
1 stick (125g) **unsalted butter**
2 **large eggs,** beaten

Finely grate the yellow part of the lemon rind, taking care not to include the bitter white pith. Halve the lemons and extract the juice – you will need 5 Tbsp.

Place the rind and juice in a heatproof bowl together with the sugar and butter. Stand over gently simmering water, and stir until melted. Add the eggs and stir until thickened – this will take about 15 minutes. Spoon into hot, sterilized jars and seal – see page 15. Store in the fridge for up to 1 month.

■ *For lime curd, use 4 limes instead of the lemons.*

Banana jam

Makes approx. 4½ cups (1kg)

3 **large ripe bananas (approx.** 12oz/350g **peeled weight)**
Juice of 2 **limes**
Juice of 1 **lemon**
4½ cups (1L) **freshly squeezed orange juice**
3½ cups (750g) **granulated sugar**

Peel the bananas and mash well, then mix with the lime and lemon juice. Transfer to a saucepan and stir in the orange juice and sugar. Heat gently, stirring, until the sugar has dissolved. Then bring to a boil and cook over a medium heat, stirring occasionally, for about 20 minutes until the syrup has reduced and turned thick and caramel-colored.

Skim off any surface foam using a flat spoon. Pour into hot jars and seal as described on page 15. Cool and store in a cool place for up to 1 month. Refrigerate after opening.

Melon and ginger conserve

Makes approx. 3 cups (700g)

1 green-fleshed melon, e.g. Galia (approx. 1lb/500g peeled and deseeded weight)
4 Tbsp freshly squeezed lemon juice
2¼ cups (500g) granulated sugar
2 Tbsp (30g) preserved ginger, finely chopped + 1 Tbsp preserving syrup

Halve the melon and scoop out the seeds. Slice off the skin and cut the flesh into small pieces. Place in a bowl and stir in half the lemon juice, sugar, ginger and syrup. Stir well, cover and leave to stand for 2 hours to allow the flavors to develop.

Transfer to a large saucepan, add the remaining lemon juice and stir over low heat until the sugar dissolves. Increase the heat and boil steadily for about 15 minutes until the syrup has reduced and thickened. Allow to cool for 15 minutes, stir to distribute the fruit pieces, then spoon into hot jars and seal as described on page 15.

Cranberry and orange sauce

Makes approx. 2 cups (500g)

2 cups (250g) fresh cranberries, washed
Scant 1 cup (200ml) freshly squeezed orange juice or water
Scant ½ cup (90g) extra-fine sugar

Put the cranberries in a saucepan and pour over the orange juice. Bring to a boil and simmer for about 5 minutes until the berries start to pop open or burst.

Remove from the heat and stir in the sugar until dissolved. Spoon into hot jars and seal as described on page 15. Cool thoroughly and store in the fridge for up to 6 weeks.

Served as a traditional accompaniment to turkey and chicken. Also good served with roast lamb, duck, goose and pheasant.

Applesauce

Serves 6 to 8 as an accompaniment; makes approx. 1½ cups (350g)

1lb (500g) **cooking apples**
2 Tbsp **freshly squeezed lemon juice**
¼ stick (30g) **unsalted butter**
3–4 Tbsp **extra-fine sugar**

Peel, core and chop the apples. Place in a saucepan and toss in the lemon juice.
Heat gently until steaming, then cover and simmer gently for about 5 minutes until
soft and collapsed. Remove from the heat and beat with a wooden spoon until
smooth. For an ultra-smooth texture, push through a nylon sieve. Stir in the butter,
and add sugar to taste. Serve hot or cold.

Served as a traditional accompaniment to roast pork, goose or duck. Also good
with pork sausages.

Oriental plum sauce

Serves 6 to 8; makes approx. 2½ cups (600ml)

6oz (180g) **cooking apple**
1lb (500g) **dark red plums,** washed
1 cup (150g) **light brown sugar**
⅔ cup (150ml) **sherry vinegar or cider vinegar**
2 **star anise**
1 **small dried red chilli**
1-in (2.5-cm) **fresh gingerroot,** peeled
1 clove **garlic,** peeled
Salt or dark soy sauce, to taste

Peel, core and chop the apples, and place in a saucepan. Halve the plums, remove the stones and halve again, then stir into the apples together with the sugar and vinegar.

Tie the star anise, chilli, ginger and garlic together in a small piece of muslin and add to the saucepan. Bring to a boil, cover and simmer gently for about 30 minutes until very soft and thick. Stand for 30 minutes then discard the spice bag.

Press the mixture through a nylon sieve to make smooth. Add salt or soy sauce to taste. Serve hot or cold.

This is a traditional accompaniment to Chinese roast duck or spare ribs. Cover and store in the fridge for up to 1 week.

Fruit coulis

Each coulis makes approx. 2¼ cups (550ml)

½ quantity **Sugar syrup (see page 144)**
1 cup (250g) **of any of the following: raspberries, blackberries, blueberries
    or strawberries,** washed and prepared, **or** 1 **large ripe mango or papaya,**
    peeled, deseeded and chopped
1–2 Tbsp **freshly squeezed lemon juice (optional)**

Make the syrup as described on page 144 and, once the syrup has cooked, add
your chosen fruit to it before it cools.

Once cold, transfer to a blender or food processor and blend for a few seconds
until smooth. Strain through a nylon sieve to make a smooth sauce. If the sauce
is too sweet, add lemon juice to sharpen. Cover and chill until required.

You can try adding extra flavorings to your chosen coulis, such as finely grated citrus
rind, vanilla extract or rosewater.

Berry vinegar

Makes 2¼ cups (500ml)

2½ cups (650g) **fresh raspberries or blackberries,** washed and hulled
2½ cups (600ml) **white wine vinegar or cider vinegar**

Place 1 cup (250g) of the berries in a non-reactive bowl and pour over the vinegar.
Cover and leave for 24 hours in a cool place. The next day, strain the liquid and
discard the fruit. Place another 1 cup (250g) fruit in a non-reactive bowl and pour over
the fruit-flavored vinegar. Cover and leave as before. The next day, strain the liquid
through muslin and discard the fruit. Put the remaining berries in a large sterilized
bottle or jar (see page 15) and pour over the fruited vinegar. Seal well and leave to
stand in a cool, dark place for at east 1 month before using.

■ *Herbs such as bay, rosemary, thyme or tarragon can be added to the final mix to add a
subtle variation of flavor, as can spices such as cinnamon, clove, star anise or mace.*

Pickled oranges and uglis

Makes approx. 2lb 7oz (1.2kg) fruit

2 large unwaxed oranges, washed
2 unwaxed ugli fruit, washed
1 bay leaf
1 cinnamon stick, broken
4 cloves
Seeds from 2 green cardamom pods, crushed
1 tsp black peppercorns
1 tsp coriander seeds
1 tsp salt
1 Tbsp light brown sugar
5 cups (1.1L) white vinegar

Slice off the tops and bottoms from the oranges and uglis to reveal the segments, then cut into ½-in (1-cm) thick slices. Remove any seeds, and place the segments in a saucepan. Add the bay leaf, spices, salt and sugar, and pour over the vinegar. Bring to a boil and simmer for 5 minutes, turning the fruit occasionally. Remove from the heat and leave to stand for 10 minutes.

Remove the citrus slices using a slotted spoon and pack into a large hot preserving jar – or you can use several smaller jars. Pour over the hot vinegar and spices and set aside to cool completely before sealing, see page 15. Keep for at least 2 weeks before eating. Store for up to 6 months. Serve with thickly sliced ham and cold meats.

Shortbread fingers

Makes 16

1 stick (125g) **unsalted butter, softened**
Generous ¼ cup (60g) **extra-fine sugar plus extra for dredging**
1½ cups (180g) **plain flour**
½ tsp **salt**

Preheat the oven to 300°F/150°C. Cream the butter and sugar together until light and fluffy in texture.

Sift in the flour and salt and gradually work into the mixture to form a soft dough. Transfer to a 7-in (18-cm) square pan and press down well to cover the bottom. Prick all over with a fork and bake in the center of the oven for about 50 minutes until pale golden. Mark into 16 fingers and dredge with extra sugar while still warm. Allow to cool in the pan completely before removing. Store between layers of wax paper in an airtight container for up to 2 weeks.

Wafer-thin ginger crisps

Makes 16

½ stick (60g) **unsalted butter**
¼ cup (60g) **granulated or** ½ cup (60g) **raw sugar**
¼ cup (60g) **corn syrup**
½ cup (60g) **all-purpose flour**
½ tsp **ground ginger**

Preheat the oven to 350°F/180°C. Line two large baking sheets with baking parchment. Put the butter, sugar and syrup into a saucepan and heat gently, stirring, until the butter melts and the sugar has dissolved. Remove from the heat and cool for 10 minutes.

Sift in the flour and ginger and mix well. Drop teaspoonfuls of the mixture onto the baking sheets, spaced about 4in (10cm) apart. Bake for about 10 minutes until golden and bubbling. Leave to cool on the trays, then store between layers of wax paper in an airtight container for up to 1 week.

Glossary

Apple

Choose apples that are sweet-smelling; they should be firm, blemish-free, bright-skinned and well colored. They are best stored in the fridge for up to 2 weeks or in a cool, airy place. Apples will deteriorate in warm conditions. They are an ethylene producer – see page 11 – so store them away from other fruit. They can also give off an odor, which may flavor other food. Only late-season apples will store over winter months, while mid-season varieties will keep only for a few weeks. When storing, the apples must be in perfect condition to start with – the saying about one bad apple can ruin a whole box is true! Wrap each apple individually in newspaper and lay in a single layer on aerated shelves or in a ventilated box. Keep in a cool, dark place and check regularly. Avoid putting different varieties in the same box.

Apple skins are a good source of beta carotene, so try to avoid peeling them. They also contain B vitamins, vitamin C, folic acid, potassium, calcium and magnesium. Apple skin also contains pectin, which can help stabilize cholesterol in the blood. Malic and tartaric acids present in apple flesh can relieve indigestion and help break down fat and protein. If you are on a low-fat diet, apples make an excellent appetite suppressant. Available all year, but best purchased locally from late Summer to early Winter.

Pear

Pears must be chosen carefully, because when they are ripe they spoil quickly; they are ethylene-producing – see page 11. Look for bright, fresh-looking skin with no bruises or damage. Pears are best bought slightly under-ripe, then stored at room temperature for a couple of days until perfectly ripe. They should yield slightly at the stalk end when ripe; pears ripen from the inside out, so waiting for softness around the middle would probably mean that the pear is past its prime. Once ripe, store in the fridge and consume as quickly as possible, bringing them up to room temperature so as to enjoy the full flavor and texture.

A good supply of beta carotene, B vitamins, folic acid and vitamin C, they are also a source of dietary fiber, potassium, calcium, magnesium and iron. Pears have mild diuretic, cleansing and laxative qualities. Available all year round, but best in the Autumn and Winter months.

Quince

The most commonly available variety looks like a large, lumpy yellow pear. Quinces can vary in size and have an intense, almost "heady" aroma. The flesh is hard with quite a few seeds and too sour to eat raw, but when cooked it develops a delicious fragrant flavor and turns from creamy yellow to pink.

Look for large, firm fruit with pale yellow to golden skin, and a smooth or downy-wool texture. Quinces store well in the fridge or a cool, dry place; choose unblemished fruit and lay them side by side, unwrapped, in a single layer on aerated shelves or in a ventilated box. Quince contains a useful amount of dietary fiber, and is a good source of potassium, calcium, magnesium and zinc. Available from mid to late Autumn through to early Winter.

Apricot

There are several varieties, differing in size, shape and color. Choose fresh and plump-looking fruit, with smooth skin and a healthy bloom. Apricots should have a good color and be free from blemishes, brown spots and bruises. They will ripen after harvest but avoid very hard fruit. They produce ethylene – see page 11 – so keep them away from other fruit and food. They will ripen at room temperature, but placing them in a paper bag speeds up the process. Once ripe they spoil quickly, so store in the fridge and use within 1 or 2 days. When perfectly ripe the skin will be soft and velvety, and the flesh deep and sweet with a central stone.

One of the best sources of natural beta carotene, apricots are also a good source of vitamin C, potassium, calcium and folic acid. Available in Summer months.

Cherry
Cherries do not ripen any further after harvesting, so select full-colored fruit. Choose plump, shiny ripe cherries with fresh green stems. Do not wash until ready to use. Wrap loosely and keep in the fridge for 1-3 days, away from strong odors, as they will be affected by other flavors. Cherries freeze well but will be soft once defrosted.

Cherries are a good source of beta carotene and vitamin C, along with vitamin B3 and folic acid. They also contain useful amounts of potassium and calcium, as well as pectin, a soluble fiber that helps to control cholesterol, and a compound that is used in the treatment of gout. Cherries are best eaten in Summer months when in peak season.

Nectarine
The name derives from its flavor – said to be like nectar, the food of the gods. It is a type of peach and not, as is often believed, a cross between a peach and a plum. Generally the flesh is yellow and the smooth thin skin is yellow flushed with red and orange. There is a large stone in the middle; this helps categorize nectarine varieties into clingstone or freestone – depending on how easily the flesh comes away from the stone.

Choose nectarines that are firm, plump and well formed; the skin should be unblemished and brightly colored, but with no signs of green. When ripe, a nectarine will yield slightly along the seam with a peachy fragrance. Ripe fruit will bruise easily, so choose slightly under-ripe ones and keep either in a warm place or in a paper bag. Once ripened, store in the fridge and keep for up to 5 days. Avoid excessively hard fruit or any with a greenish tinge. Nectarines are best frozen once cooked.

Nectarines are a rich source of beta carotene and vitamin C, with useful amounts of B vitamins and folic acid along with potassium and calcium. Nectarines have a cleansing effect on the system and can help to stimulate bowel movements. They are at their best during the late Summer months.

Peach
This is a sensuous fruit, with its soft downy skin, delicate fragrance and soft juicy flesh. As with nectarines, there are clingstone and freestone varieties, and the flesh can be white or yellow.

Choose a firm peach that yields slightly

to gentle pressure. Look for skin with a yellowy cream background color and no signs of green. There should be a light fragrance. Peaches will ripen and get softer and juicier after harvesting – ripen in a warm place or in a paper bag. Once ripened, store in the fridge and keep for up to 5 days. Avoid excessively hard fruit. Peaches are at their best during the late Summer months.

Plum
Choose good-colored, plump, fairly firm plums, as they will ripen after harvesting, Ripen in a warm place or in a paper bag. Once ripened, store in the fridge and keep for up to 5 days. Avoid excessively hard or soft fruit, or fruit that is shriveled. Plums are best cooked before freezing.

Plums contain antioxidants for boosting the immune system, and beta carotene, vitamins C and E, and folic acid. They are also a good appetite stimulant. Plums are available locally in temperate climates in Spring, otherwise they are shipped from other parts of the country or imported.

Prunes
Some varieties of plums are dried to make prunes. Available both stoned and whole, these are very sweet, with a soft molasses-like texture, and are full of dietary fiber. Prunes are a much used dried fruit and are also good cooked wrapped in bacon, in the classic Devils on Horseback canapé, or chopped and added to stuffing and sauces to serve with goose and other rich meats.

Blackberry
Blackberries won't sweeten after harvesting. If picking your own, choose a site away from road pollution or where they have not been sprayed with pesticides. Eat as soon as possible after picking and wash just before using. If purchasing, avoid juice-stained cartons, which indicate the fruit is bruised, and mold and mildew is an indication that the fruit is past its best. The fruit should be firm, dry and purple-black in color. Store unwashed in the fridge for 1-2 days, then wash well before using. Blackberries freeze well: wash, pat dry and open-freeze whole berries.

Blackberries are rich in vitamin E, folic acid and beta carotene. The leaves are a traditional cure for indigestion and purifying the blood. Availability in the wild in late Summer until the first frost. Cultivated blackberries are available pretty much all year round.

Blueberry
The blueberry is four times larger that its wild counterpart and has a refreshing balance of acid and sweet, slightly perfumed, flavors. They are blue/black in color with a silvery bloom. Look for plump berries, with a good even color and bloom. They will not ripen after harvesting, so avoid any with a green tinge or reddish color near the stem as this indicates that they are unripe. Store in the fridge for 1-2 days and wash just before using. Blueberries freeze well but do soften slightly on defrosting.

Blueberries are higher in antioxidants than most other fruit and have been hailed as a wonder food. They are a good source of dietary fiber and are rich in beta carotene, vitamins C and E, along with the minerals calcium, iron and phosphorus. Blueberries are a good overall system booster, and are available all year round.

Cranberry

The cranberry is similar to the European lingonberry, but is twice as big, though the flavor is the same. The cranberry contains a natural preservative, which allows it to be exported very successfully and gives it a long shelf life. The berries "bounce" when they are ripe. Choose bright, plump, firm and dry berries, with a bright to dark red color and uniform size. Store in the fridge for up to 2 weeks; they freeze well for up to a year.

Cranberries have a high beta carotene content and good quantities of vitamins B and C, folic acid, potassium, calcium and magnesium. They are a natural diuretic and urinary tract cleanser – the juice increases the acidity of the urine and helps destroy bacteria. Available from late Autumn through mid Winter.

Raspberry

A good raspberry will have a tart-sweet flavor and a slightly dry texture. They will not ripen after harvesting, and bruise easily when ripe. Choose plump, fresh-looking berries in good shape and full and rich in color. The berries should be dry and free from mold and mildew with no sign of juice staining the bottom of the carton. Keep in the fridge in their original container for 1–2 days, and do not wash until ready to use. Raspberries freeze well but go soft once defrosted.

Raspberries are rich in vitamin C and folic acid, and have useful quantities of beta carotene, B vitamins, dietary fiber and pectin, along with the minerals potassium, calcium, magnesium and zinc. Available all year but are at their best in mid Summer.

Rhubarb

Forced rhubarb is an early spring fruit when it is pink, thin-stalked and very tender. Later, in the summer, unforced rhubarb is much thicker, red- or green-stemmed and coarser and sourer. Select fresh-looking firm stems that are bright and glossy. Store rhubarb in the fridge for 3–4 days. It freezes well, cut into short lengths ready for stewing. Rhubarb has an intense sourness due to oxalic acid, a purgative that is harmful if eaten in excess. This acid forms mainly in the root but it also present in the stalks, though no more than in spinach. The leaves, however, contain higher amounts of this acid and shouldn't be eaten.

When cooked, rhubarb is a good source of potassium and calcium, and contains B vitamins. Available in Spring as forced, and Summer unforced.

Strawberry

Strawberries must be perfectly ripe for the best flavor. They won't ripen after harvesting, and bruise easily, so choose carefully. Look for bright red, plump, well-formed fruit with a good, even color. The berry should have a natural sheen, a fresh green cap, and a delicate sweet aroma. Remove the berries from the container and store, loosely covered, in the fridge for 1–3 days, hulling and washing just before using. Stand at room temperature before serving to allow the flavor to develop. Strawberries will freeze but they soften greatly on defrosting and become flabby, the flavor changing and losing its fresh edge.

They are rich in vitamin C and folic acid with a good supply of beta carotene, B vitamins and vitamin E, also the minerals potassium, calcium, magnesium and phosphorus. Strawberries have a refreshing, cleansing quality and act as a mild diuretic. Available all year round but the best ones are in early Summer.

Grapes

Choose well-colored, bright fruit that is plump, well-developed and firmly attached to the stalks – the stems should be green and pliable. Grapes have a natural "bloom," or slight dulling, on the skin. They won't ripen after harvesting so avoid hard fruit. Grapes wilt at room temperature so store them in the fridge for up to 3 days. Wash just before using – they are susceptible to absorbing other odors so keep away from foods such as onion. They do not freeze well.

Grapes are a good source of beta carotene, vitamins B3 and B6, folic acid and vitamin C; also the minerals potassium, calcium and magnesium. Grapes stimulate the metabolism and act as a cleanser for the digestive system and skin. If eaten with food that is slow to digest, grapes can begin to ferment in the stomach, causing gases to build up. Available all year round.

Melon

Choose a melon that is firm and heavy for its size. Avoid any that sound sloshy when shaken. Cantaloupe and netted melons will give a little at the stalk end, while winter melons are ripe when they yield to slight pressure at the opposite end from the stalk. Fresh-looking netting and a good aroma are also an indicator of ripeness. Cantaloupes and netted melons will not ripen after harvesting so avoid a very hard fruit. Winter melons, such as Honeydew, will continue to ripen as they are ethylene-producing – see page 11. Use a winter melon as soon as possible after it has ripened and store in the fridge away from other foods as the aroma may penetrate the food. Always wrap and refrigerate cut melon. Melon can be frozen in ready-prepared chunks or balls for use in salads. If you serve melon straight from the fridge it will be refreshing but have little or no flavor, so for more flavor, stand at room temperature for about 20 minutes. Melon is best prepared just before eating unless marinating.

Melons are very low in calories – the flesh is 95% water – and the juice has cleansing and diuretic properties; it is also a gentle laxative. Golden-fleshed melons are high in beta carotene; otherwise they supply potassium, calcium, magnesium and a little vitamin C. Cantaloupe and netted melons are a Summer fruit of temperate regions; at other times they may be harvested before ripening. Winter melons are available pretty much all year round.

Watermelon

Watermelon has a mildly sweet flavor, and is watery and refreshing. Many varieties exist in different shapes, sizes and colors. Look for relatively smooth, matte skin, a rounded fruit with full ends, and a paler spot where the melon has rested while growing; the melon should sound hollow when tapped gently. Avoid white streaks or spots or skin that is very shiny. Watermelons won't ripen after harvesting, so choose carefully. Store at room temperature and use promptly – if the melon gets too hot, the flesh will become dry and fibrous.

Rich in beta carotene, with useful amounts of B vitamins, folic acid and vitamin C, also potassium and calcium, watermelon is a natural cleanser and diuretic, and a natural appetite stimulant. In season throughout the Summer.

Grapefruit

The skin can vary from yellow to flushed with pink or orange, and the flesh from yellow to pink to red – the latter two being the sweetest. The flavor is sour-sweet, which gives a refreshing, slightly drying, sensation in the mouth. Choose plump, firm fruit that is heavy for its size, with smooth and firm skin. Grapefruit won't ripen after harvesting. Store at room temperature for 1 week, or in the fridge for 6-8 weeks. The fruit will be at its juiciest at room temperature. Freeze in prepared segments and use in salads.

High in vitamin C, and pink and red varieties have a rich supply of beta carotene. All grapefruit have useful amounts of folic acid, potassium and calcium. Available all year.

Kumquat

Kumquats resemble mini ovular oranges and are eaten whole, skin and pips included; they taste like sharp marmalade. Choose firm fruits with a shiny, bright color. Store in the fridge, loosely wrapped, for 2–3 days, or freeze whole for cooking.

Kumquats are a good source of dietary fibre, beta carotene and vitamin C, and also contain potassium and calcium. They are available all year round.

Lemon

Lemons come in several textures, sizes and colors: smooth to knobbly, large to small and pale to rich golden yellow. The juice is sharply acidic and the oil in the skin gives a citrus flavor and perfume. Ideally choose a fine-textured, thin-skinned lemon that is heavy for its size; look for a good deep-colored skin. The stem end is where lemons tend to show signs of aging. They are best stored in the fridge for up to 10 days. Stand at room temperature before juicing to increase yield. Unwaxed fruit will absorb odors from other foods, so store carefully. Freeze the juice and rind separately, in ice cube trays or small bags; freeze segments in ice cubes ready for drinks.

High in vitamin C, beta carotene, calcium and magnesium, lemon juice is also a good cleanser. Available all year.

Lime

The tropical cousin of the sub-tropical lemon, the lime offers a more intense flavor, is less acidic and more perfumed.

Choose plump, fresh, glossy limes, heavy for their size, with bright green skin. They can be stored at room temperature but keep them in a cool dry place, out of the sun, as this will cause yellowing; best refrigerated but keep for a short time before rind spots develop. Freeze and use as for lemons.

High in beta carotene, vitamin C, folic acid and calcium. Available all year.

Tangerine or Mandarin

The name was originally a nickname that stuck and is now a useful generic name that covers a wide range of similar fruits. It is much smaller than an orange, slightly flatter in shape; it is easy to peel and separate the segments. The flesh is sweet and less acidic than that of the orange.

Common varieties of tangerines are grown mostly in their native China and in the United States. The variety of tangerines grown in Mediterranean regions is smaller, lighter in color have a milder flavor; they have quite a lot of seeds and don't keep very long. Satsumas were developed in Japan in the 16th century. They are seedless, bright orange, easy to peel and less acidic. Tangors are a hybridized cross between a mandarin and an orange; they are smaller than an orange but similar in shape, and they have the sweeter mandarin flavor. It is thought that the clementine may in fact be a naturally occuring tangor when hybridization took place of its own accord. The minneola is a modern variety of a cross between mandarin and grapefruit. They are reddish-orange in color with a small "neck" at the top and are about the same size as a small orange. The skin is easy to peel and the flavor is distinct, rich and sharp/sweet.

Avoid dull-looking, shriveled fruit with no signs of mold or soft spots. Store as for oranges, but at room temperature for fuller flavor. They are best eaten whole, but make a good juice, which freezes well. High in vitamin C. Available from October to April in temperate zones. Minneolas are available from December to October in temperate zones.

Orange

Choose firm fruit, heavy for their size. The orange should be plump, with bright, smooth, taut skin. The color is not always a good guide, as some will stay greenish after harvesting. Store in a cool, dry place or refrigerate. Oranges give off an odor so keep them away from other foods especially eggs, meat and dairy products. Oranges are waxed for exporting, so chose organic or unwaxed ones if you want to use the rind in cooking.

Oranges are a good source of vitamin C and antioxidants. Blood oranges are also rich in beta carotene. Oranges are available all year round but are better in Winter months from Florida, Israel, Morocco and Spain.

Ugli

Belonging to the *Tangelo* family, the ugli is a cross between mandarin and grapefruit. This hybridization occurred naturally and was first discovered and patented in 1914. The fruits vary in size from those that are similar to a grapefruit to those weighing up to 2lb (1kg). The color varies from greenish mottled yellow to orange, and the rind looks like a thick, baggy sack slightly pulled up at one end. In spite of their appearance, they are easy to peel and delicately perfumed, and the flavor is low in acidity, mild and sweet.

Choose fresh-looking fruit with a good color, heavy for its size, with no signs of browning. Store as for oranges. Makes a good breakfast fruit if you don't like the acidity of grapefruit, and can be eaten halved like a grapefruit. Also good juiced.

Good source of vitamin C. Season from October to April.

Banana
Buy bananas in bunches, attached to the stalk. Look for plump, well-filled fruit with a bright even color and fresh stem. Avoid cuts, splits, bruises or soft patches. A banana that is mostly yellow with a green tip will ripen in 2-3 days. Hang on a hook away from other fruit and keep at room temperature – they produce ethylene (see page 11) and are sensitive to temperature change. If too cold the skin will split, and refrigeration causes the skin to blacken (the flesh is unaffected, although it may of course not be fully ripe). When a banana becomes very ripe the skin will be deep yellow and flecked with black or brown spots or streaks, and the flesh will be very sweet and soft; at this stage the flesh is much easier to digest.

Banana flesh discolors on slicing so prepare and use right away – otherwise sprinkle with a little lemon or lime juice to delay the browning effect.

Bananas are a good source of dietary fiber, as well as potassium, magnesium, beta carotene and vitamin B6. They also contain useful amounts of vitamin C and E. Available all year.

Date
Choose plump, soft, golden-brown fruits with smooth glossy skin. There should be no sign of fermentation. The flesh is sticky-sweet and earthy in flavor, and can be so molasses-like in texture that dates are almost a decadent alternative to a chocolate bar. Store in the fridge, but they freeze and defrost well. They contain a central stone that is best removed before eating – see page 12 – and are also available dried for baking.

They are a good energy food and are full of dietary fiber. They contain some protein, beta carotene and B vitamins. Fresh dates are available in Winter from December to February, and dried all year round.

Fig
Choose figs that are fairly soft and have a rich color and fresh smell. Avoid any with a fermenting odor, and any that are wet or excessively hard. When perfectly ripe, figs are very perishable and delicate, so either eat immediately or store in the fridge for 1–2 days. They do not freeze successfully. Depending on the variety, the flesh inside will be deep

red to orangey pink, with lots of seeds. They are sweet, with a mildly earthy flavor and gritty texture.

Figs are a good source of folic acid, beta carotene, calcium, iron, potassium and dietary fiber. They are principally available during the Summer months.

Guava

They vary in size from the size of an apple to a plum; they can be round to pear-shaped, rough or smooth-skinned, and greenish to yellow in color. The flesh inside is creamy white or pink with seeds in the center. For the best flavor, guavas are best ripened on the tree, but are usually picked before ripening for exporting. They will ripen at room temperature.

For eating fresh, choose a fruit that has slightly yellowing skin and that yields to slight pressure, but take care, as they will also bruise easily. The whole fruit is edible but it is usually peeled, and

has an exotic fragrance. The flesh has a pleasant sharp-sweet astringent flavor like a quince, and the texture is gritty with edible seeds. Simply cut in half and scoop out the contents with a spoon.

Guavas are very high in vitamin C – five times more than an orange – and also are a good source of beta carotene. They are available all year round but the peak season is late Spring to Summer.

Kiwi fruit (Chinese Gooseberry)

The kiwi fruit is about the size of a large hen's egg, with thin, brown, hairy skin that should be peeled - see page 12. The flesh is firm, green with tiny black seeds and a white central core. The flavor is slightly sweet and acid, tasting of plum and mild strawberry. Kiwis ripen at room temperature and are best eaten when slightly soft.

They are rich in vitamin C and beta carotene, and are available all year round.

Lychee

When ripe, the lychee is the size of a small plum, with reddish-brown, knobbly skin. Inside the flesh is a delicate, translucent white pulp that surrounds a large, dark, shiny, brown seed. The skin comes away quite easily if pulled with the fingers, and the seed can be removed by making a slit and pulling it out. The flavor is scented, sweet and juicy, like a muscatel grape, and very delicious.

Select firm fruit with reddish-brown skin showing no signs of decay; they keep in a bag in the fridge for at least a week.

Lychees are a good source of vitamin C and beta carotene, and are available all year round.

Mango

Mangoes can grow in size from 2in (5cm) to over 10in (25cm) long and from 3½oz (100g) to 4lb (2kg) in weight. Some varieties are round while others are long and narrow, but they generally all have a slight ridge on one side and a slightly pointed end. The skin may be yellow, orange or red, or green flushed with red and is usually removed before eating; the flesh can be pale yellow to deep orangey yellow. Mangoes have a large smooth flat central stone, which is surrounded by fibers – see page 12. The flavor is aromatic, intensely sweet, with some having a resinous fragrance and taste.

Mangoes will ripen after harvesting, either on their own at room temperature or in a paper bag to speed things up. When ripe, the fruit will yield to gentle pressure. Once ripe, store in the fridge away from other foods, for 2–3 days. Choose a plump fruit with smooth fresh skin and the desired color. Avoid mangoes that are overly green and hard, or those that are very soft and bruised. Small dark "freckles" on the skin are okay if the fruit is otherwise sound.

Mangoes are high in vitamins C, B1, B2 and B3, and beta carotene, plus the minerals calcium, magnesium and phosphorous. They are available all year round.

Papaya

This is also called Pawpaw, although this is technically quite a different species of fruit. The papaya looks like a long, large pear, and can weigh up to 1lb (500g). A ripe papaya will have yellow-orange blotchy skin and will yield slightly to gentle pressure. The flesh inside is apricot-pink in color, filled with round black seeds in the center. The flavor is delicately scented, almost peachy sweet. Because there is no acidity, papaya is often served with a squeeze of lime.

Choose a papaya that has yellow skin and is just beginning to ripen; it will continue to ripen at room temperature or in a paper bag if you want to speed up the process. There should be a gentle, fragrant aroma. Once ripened, keep in the fridge but use quickly. For preparation see page 12.

Rich in beta carotene and antioxidants, it is also a good source of vitamin C, calcium and magnesium. Available all year round.

Passion fruit
About the size of a hen's egg, the passion fruit has a purplish-brown, brittle outer shell/skin, which wrinkles and puckers slightly when ripe. Inside is an orange pulp full of seeds, which are edible and crunchy, but are often sieved to use the juice only. The flavor is strongly perfumed and a mixture of sweet and tart – a little goes a long way. Avoid any fruit that is overly smooth and greenish – it will be too under-ripe.

Store at room temperature to ripen and then keep in the fridge for 2–3 days.

The seeds are a good source of dietary fiber, otherwise the fruit is rich in beta carotene, vitamin B3 and magnesium. Available all year round.

Persimmon (sharon fruit/kaki)
There are several varieties, but the most familiar is bright orange and tomato-like in shape. It has a thin skin, which can be eaten if liked, and a stem cap at the top. The flesh is firm and jelly-like, with or without seeds. The flavor is earthy sweet, slightly astringent and tannin-rich. Strictly speaking, the sharon is a variety grown in Israel, which is seedless, coreless and lacks tannin flavor, but the name is widely misused.

Choose a plump fruit with smooth, bright and glossy skin with a stem cap still attached. The persimmon will ripen at room temperature and should be stored at room temperature and eaten as soon as it ripens. It doesn't freeze successfully.

Rich in beta carotene, potassium, vitamin C and copper, they also have a mild laxative effect. A Winter fruit available from November to March.

Pineapple
A pineapple will not ripen or sweeten once picked but gradually deteriorates, so it must kept at a carefully controlled temperature to maintain quality. Pineapples should have spiky fresh-looking green leaves at their top, and the skin is spiky with smooth flat "eyes." Color varies from greenish to golden yellow/brown – Queen pineapples often have a pinkish tinge. The color of flesh inside can vary from pale to rich golden, and the texture is juicy when perfectly ripe; the flavor is sweet and unrivaled in tanginess. The central core is woody and usually removed, but in a Queen pineapple, it is less fibrous and often edible.

Choose a pineapple that feels heavy for its size and smell the end of the fruit as an indicator of freshness. If there is any sign of fermentation, the fruit is past its best. Once perfectly ripe, the pineapple spoils quickly at room temperature, so should be refrigerated and kept away from other foods as it will taint. The juice freezes well.

Pineapple has good cleansing properties and is a good source of vitamin C. It contains lots of potassium and chlorine. Available all year round.

Pomegranate

The fruit is rounded and has thick, shiny skin that can be red, orange or bright yellow, with a small spiky "spout" at the top. Inside the fruit contains a white membrane that holds bright red juicy sacs of seeds, which sparkle like jewels. The flavor of the juice is sweet and the seeds add crunch and a tannin-rich, acidic edge; it is very refreshing. The membrane is quite bitter and should be avoided.

Choose fruit that is large and heavy for its size with a good even color. The skin should be shiny and free from cracks and splits. Large fruit will have more developed juicier seed sacs. Avoid dull, shriveled fruit. Store in the fridge for up to 2 months, and the seeds and juice can be frozen and kept for 6 months.

Rich in potassium and vitamin C, and dietary fiber if the seeds are eaten. Available all year, but at their best in late Autumn and Winter.

Star fruit (carambola)

The fruit can be up to 4½in (12cm) long and has five prominent ridges running down its length, so when it is cut in slices, each piece resembles a star. Choose a plump fruit with a waxy, deep yellow skin. Avoid green fruit, although brown edges are OK. The flesh should be sweet and juicy when ripe and the flavor is mild, reminiscent of citrus or tart apples; visually, they look fantastic. Once ripe, keep in the fridge, although they are best eaten at room temperature, and simply sliced just before using. Available all year round.

About the author

Kathryn Hawkins in an experienced food writer and stylist. She has worked on several women's magazines on the full-time staff and now as a freelancer. Kathryn enjoys using local produce in her cooking and writes on a wide range of cooking subjects. Her special interests include casual dining, regional food, cakes and baking, kids' cooking, food for health and healthy eating. Kathryn has been writing cookbooks for over a decade and has written several books on healthy eating. She is a member of the Guild of Food Writers and her ambition is to open and run her own cooking school. She is the author of *Crepes, Waffles and Pancakes!*, also published by Good Books.

Index

tropical fruit, 118–43
tropical fruit bombe,
  122–3
tropical fruit platter, 135
turkey burgers with
  cranberry relish, 73

ugli fruit, 92, 165–6
  Cuban-style candied
    citrus rind, 96
  pickled oranges and
    uglis, 156
  ugli fruit, grapefruit
    and smoked fish
    salad, 117

upside-down fruit pie,
  47

vinegar:
  berry vinegar, 155
  pickled oranges and
    uglis, 156

wafer-thin ginger crisps,
  157
watermelon, 163–4
  watermelon and crab
    salad, 90
  watermelon cooler, 91

wine:
  baked apricots with
    bay leaves, 40
  fragrant poached
    apples, 22
  fresh cherry compôte,
    44
wrinkle test, 15

yogurt:
  green melon lassi, 91
  pomegranate and
    persimmon yogurt
    drink, 139